UNDER the COVER of

KAT MARKLEY

Printed in the United States of America

ISBN 979-8-89114-201-5 (sc)
ISBN 979-8-89114-202-2 (e)

Library of Congress Control Number: 2025912610

2026.03.30

MainSpring Books
5901 W. Century Blvd
Suite 750
Los Angeles, CA, US, 90045

www.mainspringbooks.com

2010

As I sat in the doctor's office filling out the questionnaire on my current and past medical history, the question on family history of cancer or diabetes came up. As usual I had to put unknown and handed the information packet back to the receptionist, then sat back down in the waiting room to wait my turn to see the Doctor. Reading over my paperwork Dr. Bicak pronounced, (Bicheck) asked me what I meant about unknown on my family medical history, so I started to explain about how my birth parents sold me when I was approximately three years old. Sold you? He asked. Yes, I answered him. I was born in Newport Beach, California on September 15, 1959 to Anita and Ray Chapman. My birth parents sold me, two of my sisters and two of my brothers all to the same family. At this point Dr. Bicak is getting real interested and started asking questions. How do you know they sold you? Well, I replied, "I was always curious, I mean it seems everyone has family; or some form of Grandparents, Aunts, Uncles and cousins and I could not understand why no one in my family ever came forward to rescue us." I hadn't always realized the people raising us were not our birth parents or that my family was any different than any other family. Dr. Bicak was fascinated with all I had to tell him and told me, as many people before him had, that I needed to write my life story. It was fascinating but he thought it should be made into a play. If I did write it, he would be one of the first in line to buy a ticket. We finished up with my appointment, I am sure I had taken much more of his time than was my share. I went home but the memories kept coming so I decided to start writing them down and see what became of it. My first knowledge of the Myers not being my birth parents came to me by way of my siblings. They had decided that we were all going to run away. The Myers hit us for the smallest transgression not love or want us; and they were cruel, beating. They made us work all the time and we needed to find somewhere else to live. I was about six years old by this time and very confused on why they wanted us to run away from our Mommy and Daddy. My sister Sandy, who is the oldest of us five siblings and who had always taken care of us explained that they were not our real parents and that they had adopted us but did not love us or really want us and we needed to stay together. I loved my sister and did not want to be separated from her, so I went with them. Of course, our pitiful attempt at running away was thwarted because five kids walking through town carrying what few items we had, was pretty conspicuous so we were picked up and taken back to the Myers'. We were all in trouble and I remember; Mrs. Myers asking, "why I would want to run away, didn't I love them?"

Didn't they take care of me and feed me. Of course, they did all those things for me and I told her I loved her too and I did, she was the only mother I had ever known. They admitted that they had adopted us but loved us just as if we were their own. The abuse, physically, mentally, and sexually every day and because I was so young when it started, I did not understand that it was not normal. It was the only way of life that I knew. I had no knowledge of any other kind of treatment at that time and had no idea life could be different. The memories came at me in flashes of a time that I was not living with the Myers. The area we lived in was green and warm with beautiful trees and bushes. It never got cold that I can remember but we were always hungry. The neighbors had a large friendly dog that was chained to a doghouse in the back yard, and I would crawl into the doghouse, sit in there and eat his food. It was a gourmet meal to me it tasted so good! All of us children were so hungry all the time, Sandy, my oldest sister, used to sneak into our neighbors' houses and steal loaves of bread off of the counter tops or table to bring home to feed us and she would fix us oatmeal (we ate that a lot) with powdered milk. She was just a child herself and really didn't know how to cook but tried her best to take care of us. If we got bathed or our hair got combed, I'm sure she was the one to do it or it didn't get done. To this day I can't hardly stand the taste of oatmeal and forget powdered milk! We all looked like the kids you see on TV advertisements for "feed the children". Our stomachs' distended but our bodies very skinny. The ambulance came and took all of us children to the hospital, I was too young to understand what was happening, but I remember that we all got to ride in an ambulance. That part felt exciting to me.

My next memory that stands out is of Sandy and I riding in a car with two men. They came and got us after it got dark. I felt no separation pains from my birth parents at all, I guess because Sandy was with me. It seemed to be a very long ride with the men taking turns driving. Seat belts were not required apparently for I rode in the front seat on one or other of the men's laps until we reached our destination which was Arizona. We were met by Mrs. Myers, her two daughters, Sherrie who was a very large girl with red hair freckles and a terribly bad temper, you didn't want to make her mad at you, and Ginger, brown hair and freckles, always had her thumb in her mouth and was twirling her hair. The house was big and there was a lot of sand to play in, and our brother Mark was already there. Beside their house was a real big opening in the ground that was to be the basement of a house that was going to be built and we were all warned to stay away from there or we could fall in and get hurt. Mark had already fallen in once but was lucky and didn't get hurt badly. My life with the Myers was good because I had as much food as I wanted to eat, clean clothes, and I thought I was loved. It was the first parental love I had ever been shown and I wanted so badly to please them so I wouldn't be sent away. They were always correcting my speech because of the way I pronounced my words. I was told that I sounded like I was German. I was also always in trouble for the way I chewed my food. They would tell me to stop moving my mouth from side to side like a cow but to open my mouth and chew up and down. I had to really pay attention to how I chewed to keep from getting my face smacked to remind me to chew correctly. One day, we were all piled in the car traveling somewhere and I got the most awful smelling burps. I couldn't keep them in! They smelled like rotten eggs. They made me ride with my head hanging out of the window. Usually, I was way in the back, but I stunk so bad that they had to put me by the window. No one knew what caused it, and it happened on a few occasions. My sister Karen (she is one year older than me) and my baby brother Doug came to live with us some time later so all five of us were together again. During the day we played in the sand making roads for our play cars or Barbie's scraping the sand into "houses and furniture for them to sit on. I hated playing with barbie dolls but it was a way to stay together away from the Myers. We always spent hours playing outside. We tried to pick areas that could not be seen from the house so we could avoid dad, (Mr. Myers). If he saw us, he would make one of us go do a chore and the other would be left to be molested or sexually touched by him. After dark, we were fed and bathed, Mrs. Myers would come into my room and tuck me in, kiss me goodnight and make sure I had brushed my teeth and went to the bathroom because I had a problem with wetting the bed. Mr. Myers would follow a few minutes after she had left the room to tuck me in too and part of his tucking me in consisted of his touching my private parts. This happened every night and had no idea that this was not normal. As far as I knew, it was just part of the nightly routine. I had no idea that what he was doing was wrong. It was just something he did every night. Days ran into one another, nothing made one stand out from any other. School started soon enough, and I finally got to go with the older kids. I did not go to kindergarten but went right into the first grade. I don't remember too much about that time other than waking up on the school bus and being the only one on it. Apparently, I had fallen asleep on the way home from school, and no one noticed me. The bus driver made all his stops and then went back to the bus barn, parked the bus and went home for the evening.

They eventually found me and from then on one of the older kids were made responsible for making sure I got off the bus with them. It snowed one day and none of us kids had ever seen or played in the snow, so it was a big deal to see and play in it. Everyone was talking about it snowing in the desert! It didn't really feel cold out and it melted away pretty quickly.

Mr. Myers had been a construction worker and Mrs. Myers was a stay at home, mom. She did the cleaning, cooking, and kept the house in order. At some time during Mr. Myers employment, he got hurt by falling off a ladder or a roof, (I am not sure) but he did not go to work after that. They told us the whole family was packing up and moving to Kansas. Once there, we stayed at a area where cars can pull over to rest until they found and bought a large two story house at 322 South Poplar, It sat on half of a block by itself with a creek that ran behind it called the Skunk Run. The house needed a lot of repairs done but as

Mr. Myers used to work construction, he knew how to do the repairs himself.

Some of us girls shared a bedroom and the boys had to share their room too. Linda, Mr. Myers's daughter from a previous marriage, moved in with us as well with her two daughters and son so we went from a family of nine to a family of thirteen. I was no longer the youngest girl in the family. Linda's two girls, Brandy and Amy were both younger than me and Jason her son, was the same age as Doug. We had a great time playing together but children will do as children are taught. All of the sexual things that Mr. Myers was doing to us had made us more aware of our bodies and of each other's bodies too. We fought as all children will, arguing and hitting, saying and doing mean things to each other, played "doctor and house" looking at and touching each other's private parts. Not long after moving to Kansas Mrs. Myers side of the family came to visit. There was Uncle Tom, his wife Aunt Lisa and their son Pete. Uncle Jim lived with Uncle Tom and Aunt Lisa and he was my favorite. Uncle Jim was deaf, but he could read your lips and knew sign language. He could talk too but the words sounded funny when he spoke. Uncle Tom and aunt Lisa wanted to take me home to live with them because they didn't have a little girl. I really liked Uncle Jim and wouldn't have minded living with him, but Pete was mean to all of us kids and Aunt Lisa didn't think he could do any wrong. I knew he would be mean to me because he was mean while they were visiting. As an only child, he was used to getting whatever he wanted when he wanted it and he didn't like to share. I try now to remember why I didn't want to go with them, besides not liking Pete and I know now it was the fear of the unknown. I was living a life of hell, but I had my sisters and brothers and leaving them was just too scary. I needed them to be able to exist. When they tried to put me in the car to go live with them, I started crying and throwing a fit. I was scared! During my short life I had been through so many ups and downs and changes! Sandy was my lifeline. I just couldn't go live with someone else if my sister wasn't going to be there with me. They finally went home after they gave up trying to convince me what a wonderful life I would have with them. Looking back at that time, I wish I had been smart enough to have gone with them. Pete may have been mean but I wouldn't have had to go through the abuse by the Myers.

My siblings had been my only family that I knew and the thought of not having my sisters was too scary. There was a bridge that went over the creek with a big tunnel at the south end of our property and we would go into it to hide and smoke the cigarettes that we stole from Mr. Myers or one of the neighbor kids had stolen from their parents. When you crossed the creek there was an empty lot that the Myers also bought and that is where we planted a huge garden. Of course, the creek was what caught my attention! There were crawdads, snakes, worms and all kinds of fun things to catch and play with as well as the water and mud. We were made to work long hours in the garden pulling weeds or harvesting the products that were ready, We also had to use buckets to haul water from the creek to water the plants. We were allowed to plant items like Sunflower seeds that the school would pass out. Each year the school had a contest on who grew the largest sunflower. The kids would bring their largest Sunflower to school and would get to stand on the stage and show them while judges chose which ones were the tallest and had the largest flower. I remember working so hard one summer, carrying water to my Sunflowers and was so proud to take them to school when it was time. Karen, my sister that is one year older than me, begged me to let her take one since I had two that had turned out very nice. One was really tall and the other had a real large flower. I gave in and let her take one of them. It was very aggravating though because I didn't win, but she did, and she didn't tell anyone that it was actually mine. We had six peach trees on the south side of the house that we would pick for Mrs. Myers and Linda to can. We were able to eat some while we were picking them. I remember once when we were picking them, Karen took a big bite out of a really fat juicy one. When she looked at it to take another bite, there was half a worm sticking out of the peach. She got so nauseated and started throwing up; from seeing that and knowing she had just eaten half a worm. She still refuses to eat peaches to this day. Further out in the yard by the creek was a huge Mulberry tree that we put a tree house in with the help of Mr. Myers. While he was building it, he would make one of us help him and he would touch our private area and try to make us touch him. We couldn't wait till it was done so we wouldn't have to be up there with him. Many an hour was spent in that tree as children. We played fort or practiced on our curse words trying to outdo each other. We were always playing in that tree and we definitely ate our share of the mulberries. Of course, all the neighbors thought he was such a nice man to build something like that for us kids. We had two families that lived across the street that we played outside with a lot. The Gooding's and Farrar's. Both families consisted mostly of boys but that didn't bother me as I was such a tomboy. I wanted to play with the cars and trucks, cowboy and Indians and build forts. Terry Farrar was in my class and I didn't care too much for him at the time because he "liked" me, and I was not interested in boys that way yet. My sisters felt sorry for him and tried to talk me into kissing him, but I refused so they held me down on the ground and told him to kiss me. I fought as hard as I could, and every time Terry tried to kiss me, I spit in his face. It took a lot of spit, but he finally quit trying. I had a very bad habit of biting my nails extremely short, until they would bleed. Most of the time I didn't even realize I was biting them. Mr. Myers asked me one day why I bit my nails and I replied that I had watched mom (Mrs. Myers) bite hers and that is where I learned it from.

The next thing I knew, I was picking myself up off the floor from being hit so hard and he was yelling at me that my mother had never bitten her nails and don't ever say that again. Mrs. Myers stepped in at that point and told him that I must be remembering having seen my birth mother bite her nails.

I was grateful for having enough food to eat and most of the time it was good, but we were required to clean our plates. If you were served something you did not like you were made to sit there until you ate it. There were not too many things I didn't like but I have to say liver was one that I could not tolerate the taste of. It was always cooked well done and chewed like jerky with a horrible bitter after taste. When Mrs. Myers fixed that, just the smell of it cooking was enough to chase you out of the house. I would gag every time I tried to eat a bite, but it did not matter. I had to eat it. If I threw up, I had to clean it up and then sit back down and finish eating the liver. I learned to cut it into small pieces and swallow them like I was taking a pill. There were times, if you didn't eat all the food on your plate it was served to you the next morning. If you weren't eating fast enough then Mr. Myers would say show me some hurry up, ándale! Ondela! To make you chew and swallow your food as quickly as you could. Peas were my favorite vegetable at the time, so I like to take my time eating them. I got caught eating one at a time by Mrs. Myers. She told me to stop taking one pea at a time and Mr. Myers spoke up and said "don't you take one pee at a time?" Everyone laughed but she didn't think that it was funny, got up from the table, took the bowl of peas and dumped it on his head before she stormed out of the room. Linda's exhusband Bill came to see her, and the kids. He stayed for a while and she ended up taking the kids and went to live with him. I don't know where they moved to because we didn't ever see them anymore. A good memory was the Holidays! Mr. and Mrs. Myers always made Christmas special by taking us to cut down a tree, decorate it and we would get to have it up at least a couple of weeks. Christmas morning, we would get up and presents were piled under the tree with two or three gifts each. (Now I know that people in the community had adopted our family and that is where the gifts came from.) Easter time we all got to color the eggs that were boiled so we could hunt them. They boiled a lot but there were so many of us that we only got to color two or three eggs each. Once on Easter Mr. Myers called us all into the room and told us to line up. This is something that we would be made to do when we were in trouble for something that was super bad. We knew we were in for a beating. We were all so scared and wondering what we had done. Once we were all lined up, he started yelling at all of us "what we had done with the Easter baskets" that should have been there but instead there was small pieces of paper and each one had one of our names on them. Each paper had hints on where we should look the next clue. Each time we found where the paper was directing us, there would be a different note sending us a different direction. We spent quite a bit of time on the hunt because each paper gave a different clue from the previous one. We followed all the directions until we found the baskets then we would all get to go hunt the boiled eggs. Those were good days, no one seemed to get into trouble and Mr. Myers left us alone.

One day Linda and the kids showed back up and moved back in with us and her husband Bill was not with her. She was expecting a baby though and when she went into the hospital to have it, we were told that it had been a little boy she had named Chase, but he had died at birth. She and her kids lived with us from then on.

Extra room was badly needed with three adults and ten children all packed into one house, so Mr. Myers decided we needed to dig out from under the house by hand to make a basement. Once dug out it could be made into an apartment for Linda and her three kids so she could have her own space to sleep and watch television. The basement plans were drawn up and we were all ordered to put on our play clothes, go get a bucket and start carrying out the dirt that Mr. Myers was putting in them. Every day we dressed in good clothes for school but when we got home, we had to change into our "play clothes". They were usually very worn and stained so you didn't have to worry about ruining your good clothes. The boys got to wear pants or shorts but as girls, we always had to wear dresses. We all had to help every day and it was hard work. Blisters on our hands, cuts, and scratches and sore muscles. The buckets were heavy and if you didn't get them emptied as quickly as he thought you should then you took the chance of getting hit. Some of the time, not all of the children had to help. They got to go and help in the house either doing housework or laundry. The laundry was done in an old roller washing machine. Once you thought they were clean enough you had to put them through the wringers and let them drop into the container of rinse water. Then we would put them back through the wringer, dropping them into a basket.

We had to hang everything outside on the clothes lines. We decided to surprise Mrs. Myers for her birthday once and in the middle of the night, we all went to the basement and did all the laundry and had it all hung out so she wouldn't have to do it. I only lasted about half the night and fell asleep on one of the tables down there. I ended up down in the "new" basement where we were digging the dirt out, by myself with Mr. Myers and he would stop digging, pull me over to where he was, pull my panties to the side and touch my private parts. "You don't let anyone else do this do you?" "You're my girl, don't let anyone else touch you and don't tell anyone, this is our secret." The basement seemed to take forever to get dug out but finally it was all dug out. Then we had to frame and sheet rock and paint it. Linda had her own room, the girls Brandy and Amy shared one and Jason had his own room. Mr. Myers would go down to Linda's room in the basement and spend time with her without Mrs. Myers sometimes, but I had not realized at the time that he was having sex with her. We all wanted a dog and one day, we went to the dog pound and Mr. Myers said we could get a dog. We ran up and down the cages looking at all the dogs, sticking our fingers through the chain links and letting them lick our fingers. Sandy stopped and stayed by one dog and had decided he was the one she wanted, it was a large red and white dog with long floppy ears, droopy eyes and looked at you with such a sad look that you couldn't resist him. We waited to see how he acted before we picked out a name for him, but it took no time to figure that out, he just laid around, ate, drank and slept so he got the name Lazy.

I did not pass second grade the first time through. During my second year of second grade, I attended a special education class to learn how to read. Once I had gotten the hang of reading, I challenged myself to see just how fast I could read the words off and say them correctly. What I gained in speed I lost in comprehension, but I kept at it and eventually everything evened out for me as I spent as much time as I could at the library. It was a safe place for me to stay away from home and I would immerse myself into the story I was reading and escaped my true life that way. Because of the special education classes my reading skills improved, and I understood my lessons better. I made friends in school and I had started being invited by some of the girls to spend the night at their house, but I was still having problems with wetting the bed, at least part of the time so I was not allowed to spend the night anywhere else. My little brother Doug also wet the bed all the time and his hands shook extremely bad too like an elderly person would. One evening Mr. Myers had Doug and I go into the bathroom. He was yelling at us about wetting our beds and he was going to teach us a lesson so we would not do it anymore. Mr. Myers had urinated and defecated in the toilet previously and had not flushed, he reached down, grabbed Doug by the ankles, jerked him off his feet into the air, slamming his head on the floor in the process and then dunked his head into the toilet bowl as far as he could get it. Doug was crying and gagging when Mr. Myers pulled him back up and told me I was next if I didn't stop wetting the bed. I was so upset, and it grossed me out so much that I never did wet the bed again. In fact, I was one of the few that was not afraid to go to the bathroom during the night because I wasn't afraid of the dark. All the bad things that happened to me was mostly under the cover of darkness but if Ginger and Karen would wake me up and make me walk with them to go downstairs to the bathroom whenever they had to go at night. I knew I was safe from Mr. Myers. I got woke up two to three times a night after that, so it was easy to make sure I had a dry bed in the morning. Life was always terrifying, especially at night under the cover of darkness is when Mr. Myers would sneak into my room and either touch my private parts there or take me to another room to molest me. Mr. Myers would make me scratch his back but then would say I didn't do a good job because I didn't have any fingernails so he would make me sit at his feet and rub and massage them. His feet were disgusting. There was always stuff between his toes, and I had to clean that out and then use lotion and rub it into the dry flaky skin. His feet always stunk too. While he had me rubbing one foot, he would use his other foot and rub it against my private area. If I tried to move or complain, he would make me rub them longer. I spent hours sitting there rubbing his feet!

I developed a pretty tough exterior with being one of the younger kids in the family. Learning to fight or be beaten up. Most often I did not win with my older siblings, but all that practice gave me an advantage over the kids at school. My hair was real long, hitting about midthigh and it got pulled all the time. Either from fighting or when it was being combed out. There was no pain when it was pulled because I was so used to it being pulled it didn't bother me anymore.

I am ashamed today to say that I became somewhat of a bully in grade school. By making my school mates afraid of me, I made a place for myself and used that fear for acceptance. I only became mean though when I felt that someone was attacking me by calling me names or saying bad things about me. I fought one of the boys from my class right in front of the grade school because he was passing untrue rumors around school about me, he of course went straight for my hair pulling it and I doubled up my fist and belted him right in the mouth so hard his teeth split the knuckles on my hand. He never came back to school but I had made a name for myself as someone not to be messed with and kids wanted to be my friend so I wouldn't beat them up. They Myers took away my crowning glory though by taking me to the beauty parlor one day and telling me they were getting my beautiful blond hair cut off because I didn't take care of it or keep it combed like I should. The beautician cut off my hair up by my ears calling it a "pixie" cut. To me it just looked like someone put a bowl over my head and cut around it. The beauty salon had my hair made into two wigs and I got to see them when they were done. They were beautiful and were shoulder length. My hair started turning a darker color than it had previously been, and my blond locks were gone. It was easier to take care of though and didn't take near as long to comb out or to wash.

Physical abuse was a constant threat at our house. Punishment for any infraction, real or imagined would incite yelling at, being hit, degraded, stood in a corner or sent to bed with no supper. You never knew when or what the next punishment would be for or how severe it would be. It seemed to us that Mr. Myers tried to find reasons and ways to punish us that he got some kind of enjoyment out of it. We swore, that he hid his own tools and then would start yelling at everyone wanting to know where they were, which one of us had taken and lost them. When none of us were able to answer his questions, (and he knew we wouldn't be able to) he would get madder and would make us all line up from oldest to youngest and would again ask which of us had lost the tool. When he did not get a confession, he would start down the line hitting us with a leather belt, a switch off of a tree, a board or a piece of rubber hose, whatever was within his reach. Once he used a portion of a garden hose, hitting the back of our bare legs until one of Karen's legs split open like it had been cut. There was a cuckoo clock hanging on one of the walls that I was fascinated with and was always watching. I don't know why it fascinated me so much, but it did. Something about that bird coming out and making a noise just fascinated me. The clock came up broken one day and I was called into the living room and questioned on how I had broken it. It had to of been me as I was always the one looking at it and no matter how hard I tried to deny that I had broken it they would not believe me.

I was beaten with the leather belt so hard I had welts on the back of my legs for hours. Part of my punishment was for breaking the clock the other part was for lying about it. When we became adults Jason (Linda's son) admitted that he was the one that had broken the clock, but he was too terrified to admit it at the time.

Mr. Myers touching is getting bolder; it wasn't just at bedtime anymore. It was happening if he caught me in the garage, the basement or any room when I was by myself. Then the slimy kiss was added to the nightly goodnights. We were required to kiss Mr. Myers goodnight before going to our rooms to sleep and if we did not do so we would get in big trouble. By trouble I mean you didn't know if you would just be yelled at, or a fist or a hand would slam into you, upside your head hard enough you would see stars. We suffered the kiss. He would pucker up his lips into what seemed to me like an open square shape, place them over your lips and slime you with his tongue. You didn't dare wipe it off either as I did once, or you would pay for that infraction by either having to suffer through another one or being hit. We learned to be sneaky and as soon as we were out of sight, we would scrub off our mouths with our night gowns, hand, arm, or whatever was handy as quickly as possible to keep from gagging. He would soon follow to start the nightly tucking and touching. This had really started to give me an uncomfortable feeling, but I thought that this was normal and what all daddy's did. When we went on family outings to the lake, he would come out to play with us kids. He would take me into deeper water and touch my private parts under the water where it could not be seen, pull his penis out the leg of his swimsuit and rub it against me. Mrs. Myers didn't swim so she never went into the deep water. Mr. Myers was so daring in his sexual pursuits that he would send all the kids out of the living room where we would all be watching television while Mrs. Myers and Linda were in the kitchen cooking, except me. After everyone had left the room, he would unzip his pants, pull me onto his lap, move my panties to the side and rub his penis against my private. When Mrs. Myers or Linda would yell out that supper was ready, he would pull my undergarments back in place, tuck his penis back in, zip up his pants and go into dinner like nothing had happened.

It also meant that I was getting old enough to spend the night at a friends' house. I was so excited by being invited to Glenda's house! Her family seemed to be so nice, always so polite and kind and they invited me to go to church with them the following Sunday too. Her mom and dad wished us a good night from the doorway when it was bedtime and it struck me as odd that her dad didn't tuck her in like mine did me. I asked Glenda about it and she was amazed at my questions and answered that her dad never did that. That was my first insight to not all families were like mine and that and the uncomfortable feeling I had when my dad was doing it was normal. I had such a wonderful time spending the night at Glenda's house that when Glenda had invited me to the Halloween party at her church I very much wanted to go. I asked permission from Mrs. Myers to go but she said,"what did your father say?" so I had to go ask him and he said "what did your mother say?" I told him that she said to ask him, then he said "It is ok with me if it is ok with her" so off I went to tell Mrs. Myers what Mr. Myers had said and then she said "it is ok with me if it is ok with him" so I took that to mean I could go. I went to Glenda's house after school ate dinner with her family and then her dad took us to the Halloween party. It was so much fun! There was bobbing for apples and all kinds of games being played, music, snacks and punch. Everyone was dressed in costumes and having a great time. I had never been to or experienced a Halloween party like that. When the party was over, Glenda's dad took me back to my house. The Myers were waiting for me and as soon as I entered the house, they ask "where have you been young lady?!!" I was confused by this question as I had asked permission to go to the party but answered that I had been to the Halloween party with Glenda and her family. They asked, "who gave you permission to go to the party?" and I said, "you both did," that Mr. Myers said that it was ok with him if it was ok with you and you said it was ok if it was ok with him, so I thought that I was allowed to go." Mr. Myers yelled at me and said "that was not giving you permission to go, you just took it on yourself to do as you wanted, then started hitting me with a leather belt. When he was done hitting me, he yelled that I was grounded and sent me up to my room. The Myers had some friends over to visit and all the children were sent upstairs to play. One of them was a boy about my age and of course we played you show me yours and I will show you mine. My older siblings were daring me and trying to get me to touch his penis. I didn't want to, but they kept trying to get me to and he had unzipped his pants so when one of the adults had come up to check on us and see why we were being so quite they saw his pants unzipped and they figured out pretty quick what was going on and made us go downstairs to face the adults. We were in so much trouble! I tried to tell them that I had not done what they thought I had but no one would believe me till the little boy finally admitted that I had not participated. The guests left with their children and I was still in trouble along with the other kids because I had not gone downstairs and told on them. We never saw that family again. That incident seemed to give Mr. Myers the idea that I was ready for him to go a little further in his touching. He started putting his finger partially inside me when he was touching my private parts. I didn't like it, would cry and asked him to stop. It did no good; he didn't stop until he was ready to. I fought with all my strength but it was no match for a large grown man. Once I work out from fighting him it's almost as if I would depart my own body until he finished what he was doing.

I would lie there as if I were no longer present. I started trying to avoid him, sleeping at a friend's house, spending as much time as possible at the library or have a friend stay at our house because he didn't bother us when we had company stay over. If all else failed, us girls would sleep in the same bed in the hope that he would leave us alone. Mostly he would do this at night but was getting braver and started touching me during the day too. Putting it all together, being lined up for the beatings, the sexual touching and kissing and understanding that it was not normal, that other families did not treat their children this way, I wanted to have a family like my friends had. My sisters and I had talked, and we were now aware that Mr. Myers was sexually abusing all of us. If he did not get his way, he would get angry and a few times he caught me by myself and said he had looked for me the previous night and that I had better be in my bedroom the following night when he came to find me. He would then take my hand in his and rub his middle finger in the palm of my hand. I had no idea what this meant or what it did for him, but I soon learned that it boded ill for me. There were times when we girls slept in the same bed, he would wait for us to go to sleep, come in during the darkest part of the night and steal you out of the bed, take you to an empty room to get his sexual fix.

Mr. Myers was always working on one construction project or another and at least one of us was required to help him. When he asked you to hand him a certain tool, you needed to hand him the right one and place it in his hand, with the handle in his palm, facing up ready to use. If this did not happen you could count on having the tool thrown at you, being yelled and cursed at and most likely being hit. Then you would be made to rehand him the tool correctly. While he was working on a plumbing job in the basement, I had to help him, he asked me for a certain wrench. I didn't know which wrench it was so I picked the one I thought it might be and handed it to him. Of course, it was not the right one. I had given him a crescent wrench. In his anger at my not handing him the correct wrench he threw it at me. It was summertime so I was barefoot, and the open mouth of the crescent wrench embedded into the top of my left foot. Then I got cussed out for being barefoot and I deserved what I got for not wearing shoes. When the job was completed, he pulled me over to him and hugged me, rubbed my back and then slid his hand into my panties touching me and told me I was his girl. Sometimes he wouldn't ask for what he wanted but other times he would just stare at an object and we had to guess at what he wanted. He would do the same thing at the dinner table, just stare and everyone would be trying to hand him what they thought he was looking at. We always had to make sure that when you set the table that his place setting at the head of the table had his favorite plate, knife, fork and spoon. He would not use any others and if they were not there, the table setting would be knocked off the table and you would be scrambling to get the right ones.

Though life was difficult for me, it seemed like Mr. Myers was even harder on the boys, Mark, in particular. Mr. Myers would call Mark names like "nigger" and "black son of a bitch" because Mark's skin was dark, his hair was black and curly, but it was silky soft curls, not kinky, his features could be considered African American. From what Sandy says, Mark was of Indian heritage and with her being the oldest, myself and my siblings all believed her. Mark was always getting beat for one reason or another, he didn't have to do anything to warrant being hit or knocked about. Ginger had a tendency, to break her arms easily and while we were all outside playing, she fell and broke her arm again for the seventh time! Mark was the closest to her location when she fell so Mr. Myers went after him for letting her fall. Ginger did her best to tell

Mr. Myers that it was not Mark's fault that he didn't have anything to do with it, but he would not listen and beat Mark until he was on the ground then proceeded to kick him in the stomach and face with his boots on. Several of Marks front teeth were kicked out by the roots. His teeth were so badly damaged that the Dentist could not put them back in. Mark tried to run away after that, but the police brought him back. Even with the split lip and bruising on Mark, Mr. Myers was able to convince them that Mark was lying, and no one had abused him, that he was a troublemaker, and was always getting into fights.

The Myers actually allowed us to attend the Seventh Day Adventist church, but we had to walk there or rely on a fellow Christian to give us a ride. The service was held on Saturday and it provided us a way to escape the Myers for a few hours. Neither of the Myers or Linda attended but all of us kids did. We felt the love, acceptance and welcome from the people there. It didn't matter that we didn't have new clothes or that we didn't have money. No one yelled at us there and we were made to feel as if we belonged. Two women who were especially kind were Barbara and Donna. They were sisters, each married with children of their own but always found time to make us feel special. They would ask us to help with the bible class we were in by reading out loud, leading in song (I loved to sing) or to help a younger child with whatever project they were working on. We were also invited to go to summer camp for a week during the summer. It cost money and we didn't have any so the church would hold car washes, bake sales and would ask for extra donations from the congregation to help the less fortunate children go. It was wonderful! Children were separated into groups by age and sex and then assigned to a cabin with a college student or two to stay in the cabin with you and be in charge of your activities. We would all go to the main house to eat and they had a little store off to the side of it that you could buy candy, chips, soda, stamps and envelopes. After eating breakfast, we would go to the lake and were shown how to canoe and were able to swim and play in the water then go eat lunch. Horse riding in the afternoon, every afternoon! I had never been on a horse before but discovered I loved riding! The horse I got to ride was so tall and my counselor said he was fifteen hands tall (that made no sense to me) but I didn't care. He was fun to ride and followed the leaders without me having to do anything but sit on his back, enjoy the scenery, soak up the sun and relax. On our first day back from the trail ride my horse figured out where we were going, and he stopped following the leader and took off at a trot instead of his slow walk he had been doing. The counselor told me to pull back on the reins and I was pulling with all my strength, but I could not pull hard enough to get him to slow down.

He started running at a full out gallop and all I could do then was hold on, bouncing up and down on the saddle as he headed straight for the truck and trailer jumping over where the tongue of the trailer connected to the truck. I managed to stay on, and he slowed and then stopped when he got to the barn. Everyone was crowding around me, pulled me off the back of the horse asking if I was ok. It had been pretty scary at first, but it had also been exciting. I liked getting all the attention from everyone.

I had the coolest councilor! She was very short, (I was almost as tall as her), shoulder length blond hair and was a college student, volunteering at the camp for the summer with some of her friends. Her name was Collett and she let me hang out with her and the older kids. She was so easy to talk to, I told her about my life and what was happening to me. She was shocked when I told her what Mr. Myers was doing and so understanding. She wanted to help me, but she did not have the knowledge or ability to do anything but try and make my stay there the best that she could by including me in with things the councilors did when they weren't working with the children. I think she saw how desperately I needed someone to just care about me with no strings and no expectations. I was so hungry for someone to love me for who I was. I hated it when camp week was over, and I had to go back home. That was the only time in my life that I actually felt free and unafraid.

When Mr. Myers would need to go to the hardware store or junkyard to get a part or pick something up, he would make one of us girls go with him. He would make us sit right next to him while he was driving and then slide his right hand into your panties, saying things like "you like that don't you; that feels good doesn't it; you don't let any other boys, or your brothers touch you like this do you?" "You are mine so don't let anyone else touch you here." He would grab my hand and try to make me rub his penis through his pants. On some of the trips he would pull off on a country road, unzip his pants, take his penis out and try to get you to touch it. I would not do it, so he took my hand in his and made me touch it. I thought it was hot to the touch and tried to pull my hand back, I didn't want to do that and resisted even at the threat of making him mad and possibly getting hit. It was big, ugly and leaked and I wanted nothing to do with it. Trying to fight him off did no good so I would just disappear in my mind. All of us girls got together and had a meeting about what Mr. Myers was doing and decided between ourselves that we needed to approach Mrs. Myers about it. Sandy said that she had told Mrs. Myers once that Mr. Myers was sexually abusing her, but he denied it, said she was lying and had made it all up, the abuse had not stopped. We decided it was worth approaching her again with all of us going to her together so she would know that we were telling the truth. I discovered during our meeting that Mr. Myers had never touched Sherrie or Ginger the way he had been touching us and figured it was because they were his biological children while we were not. That was when I found out that Sherrie and Ginger were not Mrs. Myers real daughters but Linda's. Mr. Myers had had sex with Linda and gotten her pregnant twice. That was the agreement between Mrs. Myers and Mr. Myers before he married her because she couldn't have anymore children. Sherrie and Ginger were the results and Mrs. Myers took them and was raising them as her own daughters.

We approached Mrs. Myers and told her what Mr. Myers was doing and she got very upset, told us she was sorry, cried and hugged us all promising that she would talk to him about it and that we didn't need to worry because he wouldn't bother us anymore. They had a terrible argument about it screaming and yelling with her accusing him, and him denying that he had ever touched any of us. It was pretty scary and uncomfortable at our house for a quite some time, but he did stop touching me for a little while anyway. Things eventually calmed down between them and he was being very nice to her, so she let her guard down and the touching started happening again. This time there were threats of you had better not tell your mother or else! He was a very large man and to a little girl that had already been abused so much by him, I was too terrified to say anything to anyone about it for a long time.

Life went on and there was always one project or another going on. Mr. Myers got a load of used bricks from somewhere. We all had to clean the old cement off of them (without breaking them) and stack them, so they were ready to be used to make surround walls for flower beds. Sandy and Sherrie were super close in age and always hung out together. They were working on the bricks facing each other when they both started messing around acting like they were going to toss their hammer at each other. Sandy's hammer slipped out of her hand one of the times she thrust her hammer at Sherrie. It hit Sherrie in the mouth. Sherrie grabbed her mouth and ran for the house with Sandy and Mr. Myers on her heels. Mr. Myers was yelling at Sandy and was going to beat her with the belt, but Sherrie stopped him by yelling right back that they had both been playing around and it had been an accident. She was really mad at Sandy but knew that she had not meant to hurt her. Sherrie seemed fearless to me when she stood up to Mr. Myers!

Part of our daily life was the constant sexual approaches from Mr. Myers and no matter how hard I tried to thwart his advances he found ways to get to us. This went on for several years before we felt that we could not put off telling Mrs. Myers again. She was furious partly at us because we hadn't told her right away when it had started again and at him. She confronted him in the living room and had us all right there when she did it. He was instantly extremely angry and denied it saying we were liars, making it up, she didn't love him anymore because she was taking our word over his. His hammer was hanging from his tool belt, he grabbed it and slammed the claw part of the hammer into her left shoulder. She fell like a ton of bricks and we all just stood there stunned. No one could believe what had just happened and then there was total chaos. Everyone started crying, we were all scared and then we were chased from the room with him yelling at us "see what you made me do!" He tried to cover up what he did by taking the hammer and throwing it through the picture window. Mr. Myers and Linda then wrapped her shoulder in towels and took her to the hospital. We were all instructed to say that during an argument they were having Mr. Myers, in anger went to throw his hammer at the window and she stepped in front of it. The police did come to the house, talked to Mr. Myers, looked around, made out a report and that was the last we saw of them. He didn't get into any trouble at all over what he had done to her.

During the time Mrs. Myers was in the hospital was not a good time for any of us. Mr. Myers was angry (and I think scared that someone would find out that he had hit Mrs. Myers with the hammer on purpose) blaming us for her injury. Linda was also mad at us because she thought it was our fault that her mother was in the hospital hurt and we were all worried that Mrs. Myers was going to die. Mrs. Myers had her times that she could be mean, calling us names like hussy and slut (I didn't know what they meant but by the way she said them I knew they were bad). She would tell us we were no good and came from trash so we would never amount to anything and would always be white trash. Did we know what luxuries Sherrie and Ginger had given up, so we had a place to live as well as dole out the slaps and call us horrible names. The worst punishment she gave out though was the one when she said wait until your dad gets home. That was terrifying and I would be sick to my stomach with fear by the time he walked through the door because I knew how much worse the beating with the belt would be. She was also the one that fed us, clothed us and provided the good kind of kisses and hugs, taking care of us when we were ill or hurt and the only mother I had ever known and no matter how many times she hurt me, I still loved her. I tried helping with the housework by sweeping the floors or dusting. Anything to try and please her.

One of the nights that Mrs. Myers was in the hospital Mr. Myers came to my bedroom, picked me up out of my bed and carried me to their bedroom, then closed the door behind himself. He placed me onto the bed, I noticed there was a towel on the bed, and he crawled onto the bed with me and laid me on the towel. Then he started removing my pajamas. He started touching and kissing my budding breasts and then removed my panties while I struggle with him to keep them on. I tried to squirm away and told him that I didn't want him to touch me. He hushed me saying that I needed to be quiet, gripped my arms roughly to hold me in place and told me to stop fighting him. Taking my panties off, he then started touching my private parts rubbing up and down and inserting his finger part of the way into my vagina. I'm fighting him as hard as I can, but I don't stand a chance. He took my hand and placed it on his engorged penis wrapping my fingers around it with his own. He said he liked that and to keep moving my hand on his shaft when he removed his hand but as soon as he let my hand go, I moved it away. He took my hand and placed in on his penis again and didn't let go this time until it was starting to seep. Talking to me the whole time on how good it felt continuing the movement up then down while he is still touching me with his other hand. He finally released my hand and I moved it away from him. Then he used both his hands to spread my legs apart and moved on top of me then reached down with his hand, gripped his penis placed the head against my private and started rubbing it up and down my opening a few times then proceeded to push his penis against the opening of my vagina. I started crying and begging please stop daddy it hurts, please stop it hurts, it hurts but my cries and tears were ignored, and he did not stop until he all of a sudden pulled out and some liquid coming out of it landed on my stomach. At the tender age of eight, my innocence was violently stolen. My innocence was gone, stolen from me before I even knew what it meant. Much later in my adult years my brother Mark told me that he had heard me crying and begging Mr. Myers to stop, and that it hurt but he was not old enough or strong enough to fight him and help me.

The day arrived that Mrs. Myers came home from the hospital. We were all so excited that she was home but when she arrived, she still looked very ill. Her complexion was chalky, and she seemed to be weak and shaky. She seemed quieter than before she was hurt and once she healed enough to get out of bed, she did not act or talk like she did before. Now she seemed afraid to say or do the wrong thing, to make Mr. Myers mad. It seemed all the fight had gone out of her but now I realize she was just as afraid of him as we were and could not protect herself, anymore, then she could protect us. When Mr. Myers approached us now with his sexual advances the warnings admonished were even more stern, "don't tell your mother unless you want to be responsible for killing her or it would kill your mother if she knew what you and I do, and you don't want to hurt your mother do you? Don't tell anyone or I will make you sorry you were ever born" and by the look he was giving you, you knew he meant every word he was saying. On some of the occasions that I was forced to go with him, he pulled onto a dirt road and parked off to the side. He got out and came over to the passenger side and made me lay down on the seat. He grabbed me and scooted my butt to the edge of the seat and molested me right there.

Mr. Myers bought Mrs. Myers a puppy, a male Pekinese because she wanted one and he was still trying to get on her good side. After seeing the puppy, Linda decided she wanted one too and got a little female. They had decided that way they could breed them and sell the puppies. The puppies were registered, and Mr. Myers decided he needed a fancy name to put on the paperwork, so he named him Qulis Tongis Hongis Congis Dingis Dongis. We thought his flat nose and the way it always looked like he was bumping it when he smelled something that his name should be bumper and that is what we called him. We all loved bumper he was so cute and loved playing with us. One of the days I was attending school I noticed that the urge to go pee was all of a sudden so urgent that I could not make it in time and peed my pants. Of course the other kids made fun of me and I was so embarrassed and scared I didn't want to tell any of the adults. The urge to pee was frequent and when I would go it hurt and very little urine would come out. I was too afraid to tell anyone what was wrong and went through several days of having to pee frequently and then having pain when I did but eventually it went away and so did the hurting sensation. I don't remember being taken to a doctor or taking any kind of medication for the problem but that it just went away on its own.

Now that Mr. Myers had started having intercourse with me it seemed like he was constantly molesting me. Any excuse to get me alone or he would sneak into my room at night, it did not seem to matter to him. Mrs. Myers was no longer a source that I could go to for protection. By this time, I had started having my monthly menstrual and was extremely embarrassed when Mrs. Myers brought Mr. Myers up to my room to announce to him that I was now a woman. He congratulated me and came over to give me a slimy kiss and a hug. Now I not only had to worry about being raped but of getting pregnant by him! If we tried to tell her, like she said we were to, then she blamed us. We were the ones leading him on. You're just a little hussy and it's your fault he does that she would sneer in a hateful and hurtful voice.

We tried several times to run away, sometime together and sometimes by ourselves, but we were always caught either by the police, someone the Myers knew or even by the Myers themselves. We would get a terrible beating each time we were caught and taken back and would be grounded. The community thought the Myers were saints for taking in and adopting five children and that we should be more grateful for all they had done for us, and stop being such troublemakers. By fifth grade I had accepted my life as it was and had mellowed out for the most part. I didn't get into fights anymore, was a cheerleader for the grade school football team and was liked by most of my classmates. I was noticing boys at school, but not only did I admire or have a crush on them, but I was probably more sexually aware of them as well. That is what I knew so it was only natural for me to have those kind of feelings and thoughts. I never let anyone know what I was feeling or thinking though because I thought, "those kind of feelings", were dirty and bad. When Mr. Myers would come to my room at night now, sometimes the touching would feel good, but I knew it was wrong and bad, so I had very mixed feelings. I still did not want him to touch me or have intercourse with me and I still resisted, fighting him off as much as I could but my puny strength against a grown man amounted to nothing to him. Mrs. Myers' mother came to live with us because she had gotten too old to take care of herself. I loved Grandma! She always had time to hold me, talk to me, and she never yelled at or hit me. I would sit for hours and play with the skin on her hands. I could pinch it lightly and it stayed in that position. The attention she was willing to give us was unending and she never seemed to run out of patience. Grandma had trouble remembering things, like if she was cooking and would get sidetracked easily, she would forget all about it and it would end up burning so she wasn't allowed to cook though she could help prepare things like peel potatoes, snap green beans, small chores like that. Grandma needed assistance with some things and one or other of us children were always ready to help her with anything we could. We could not help with bathing or dressing her though, that was a chore only Mrs. Myers or Linda could help with. Grandma was getting worse with her memory and abilities though and one day she came out of her room with her dress on inside out. Mr. Myers yelled at Mrs. Myers and told her to get her ass in there and dress her mother right before the neighbors saw her. We could hear Mrs. Myers yelling at grandma, hitting and slapping noises were also coming from her room. Grandma was being beaten for not knowing how to dress herself and making Mr. Myers mad. I felt so bad for grandma and I could not help her other than let her know I still loved her when she came out of her room. I sat and held her hand for hours. Poor grandma tried but it seemed the worse she got the more often she was being beaten. She passed away in her sleep one night escaping the nightmare her life had become.

Sandy is gone! We are told that she is a whore, that she is pregnant and has moved in with her boyfriend and his family. We were not to have anything to do with her anymore and that she was no longer a part of our family. I am ten years old (almost eleven,) and that made Sandy fifteen and she was going to be a mommy. I missed my big sister so much and yearned to be able to see and talk to her, but she had made her escape from Mr. Myers and I was happy for her! I heard from a friend that Sandy was working at the day care center in the church right across from the library I spent so much time in so I tried to watch for her to see if I could see her since they Myers had forbid any of us to have any contact with her. One day it paid off. An older lady and Sandy came out of the church with a row of small children all holding onto a rope to walk to the park. I ran over to talk to her and give her a big hug. It was so great to see her, and she seemed happy to see me as well. She said that Allen (her husband) and her were living with his mom and dad until they could get on their feet and that she would be having a baby in August. I snuck over to see her every once in a while, after that; but not too often because I didn't want to get caught or get her in trouble. Sandy had a little boy that she named William Allen, but they called him Little Allen after his father. She let Mrs. Myers know when he was born, and Mrs. Myers went to see her and the baby. Mr. Myers still wouldn't have anything to do with her, but we were allowed to see her again without fear of getting caught. Her husband Allen had decided to join the army and she stayed with her inlaws until he was out of basic training before she could join him in Germany with little Allen. I no longer had her to talk to, I had to face my problems on my own.

Mr. Myers, dad and step mother lived in Kansas City and we all of a sudden started visiting them. We had never met them before but all of a sudden, we were visiting them. Their house was in an old neighborhood and all the houses were really close to each other. There were no garages or driveways, you parked in front of the house and then had to go up a tall flight of stairs to get into the house. On one of our visits, grandpa was talking to Mr. Myers and said he had stubbed his big toe. He took off his sock and showed it to us, it was all black. Being a diabetic, he did not heal easily and the damage he had done to his toe had gotten infected. Mr. Myers told him he needed to get to the doctors and have him look at it. The next thing we knew grandpa was living with us. The doctors had cut his leg off just below his knee because gangrene had set in and they could not save his foot. He was wheelchair bound and could no longer get in and out of his house and grandma was too old to take care of him, she didn't want him to come back. It was nice having grandpa around, he would show us his "stump" and talk about how his foot itched, but he couldn't scratch it. We thought that was really strange because his foot wasn't even there! Grandpa would hold us on his lap and spend time talking to us and was very generous in money. We all got a small allowance every week to spend and one week, we were given a little more than usual from Mr. Myers. We didn't know why but thought it was great! At dinner time, we figured out why. It was Ginger's birthday and he had given us extra money so we could get Ginger a birthday present. He didn't mention at the time he gave us the extra money that it was her birthday. We just thought he was being extra nice. We had never bought each other gifts and none of us knew it was her birthday. At dinner time, we were told it was her birthday and we were going to have cake and watch her open presents after dinner. Mr. Myers asked us what we had bought Ginger for her birthday and we all said nothing. We had spent the money that he gave us on candy. None of us kids had ever bought birthday presents for each other, so I was surprised by this question. Mr. Myers told me how selfish we were, thinking only of ourselves and what candy we had left, we had to give to Ginger.

The announcement that grandpa was not allowed to give any of us any money and more was made at that time, the money would be put to better use by helping to pay the bills. From then on grandpa never got any of his money and if he asked about it, he was told he had no need for it, they fed and clothed him, put a roof over his head and his money was paying for that. If grandpa tried to argue about it, Mr. Myers would hit him so hard that sometimes he would fall out of his wheelchair. Grandpa got to where he couldn't lift or support his own body weight so was unable to go to the bathroom by himself. He had to rely on Mr. Myers to help him. If he could not hold it until Mr. Myers was able or willing to help him and wet of defecated in his pants Mr. Myers was the one that had to clean him up and he would beat Grandpa severely. The summer before my sixth grade year, grandpa passed away. Mr. Myers Some of the teachers were finally starting to listen and believe us about being abused. Mr. Myers was thought very highly of in the community. He led the Ekan team that helped the under privileged with Housing and food. They had seen too many of us come through their classrooms and had heard the same stories from all of us about being hit and touched in our private parts. Questions are being asked and people are getting suspicious. One of the teachers that was asking questions and trying to help us ended up losing her job over it. Not long after that the Myers started talking about selling out and moving again.

The house sold and we all had to pack up our belongings, load them into a uhaul trailer to move back to Phoenix Arizona. While we were trying to pack and load everything Sherrie announced to the Myers that she was pregnant too and wanted to marry her boyfriend, Roger. The Myers were furious and started yelling at her about how she was a whore just like her sister Sandy. Sherrie had not run away to her boyfriends, house though like Sandy had and they did not let go of her so easily. She was told that she still had to move with them, and that Roger could come too. Roger could drive the station wagon so Mr. Myers wouldn't have to haul it because neither Mrs. Myers or Linda knew how to drive. Roger agreed to do this, and we headed for Arizona. None of us girls wanted to ride with Mr. Myers because we knew what he would do but we were not always able to get out of it. He would make one of the other of us ride with him and would make us sit right next to him, so he had access to your private parts.

We stopped at a truck stop to eat breakfast one of the mornings then got back on the road We had been traveling for a few hours when Mr. Myers pulled over to get gas for the truck and station wagon and to let everyone go to the bathroom when Mrs. Myers realized she did not have her purse. We all looked everywhere but it was not in the car. She remembered taking it into the truck stop and still had the receipt with the phone number on it so went inside and called but were really worried if someone had turned it in, all the money would be gone. Someone had found her purse and taken it to the cashier, and they were holding it in front for her. They left us kids with Linda and drove back to the restaurant to get it and when they arrived to retrieve the purse all the money was still there. When we would stop at night we had to crowd into the seats of the different vehicles and the back of the station wagon to sleep. I was in the same vehicle as Sherrie and Roger and could hear them having sex and talking in whispers about hoping that she got pregnant this time. Sherrie had lied to the Myers about being pregnant because she did not want to leave Roger and wanted to marry him.

During the move, the station wagon had a flat tire. We had to pull over to the side of the road to change it. Mr. Myers jacked the car up to change the tire not realizing how much of a slope it was parked on and the car started to roll over onto its side. Mr. Myers started shouting push! Push! I was on the opposite side of the car that it was leaning toward and started pushing like I was being yelled at to do so I did. It did not occur to me that I was pushing on the wrong side, that I needed to be on the other side to help keep the car from rolling, not that my puny efforts really could have made that much difference anyway. When they got the car held in place and the car lowered some, Mr. Myers turned to me and yelled at me for being such a God Damned idiot as to push on the wrong side of the car. He threw the tire iron at me and it embedded into the top of my left hand just below my pinkie finger, when I threw it up to protect my face from being hit. My hand swelled to twice it's normal size, got infected and took forever to heal. Once it did heal, I was left with an inch long scar on my hand but that was still better than if it had hit me in the face. After getting on the road and going again until nightfall, we stopped beside the road to spend the night. When we were almost to Arizona, the Myers figured out that Sherrie had been lying about being pregnant and there was a big yelling and screaming fight between them. I don't know how they found out, but my thoughts are that she got her period. They finally gave in and let Sherrie marry

Roger at a justice of the peace and they left to go back and live with Roger's parents until they could get a place of their own.

We moved out into the desert of Phoenix, houses were far and few between and camped out there. Mr. Myers had decided that he was going to build our house himself. We had no running water, so he had to buy a tank that would fit on the back of the truck. Electricity was finally run to the property we were camping on. No bathroom or kitchen or any normal house hold items. When we had to go to the bathroom, we had to find a bush or sand dune to go behind always keeping an eye out for scorpions or rattlesnakes.

Mr. Myers used the tank to haul water in, a big wash tub for us to bath in but the water had to be heated over an open fire, so we all had to share the same tub of water. The older kids got to go first and then down the line by age. Sometimes the water was pretty murky by the time it was my turn. Mr. Myers dug a deep hole in the ground and built a small room around it with a door on one side and a bench seat inside that he had cut a hole in. That was our new bathroom that he called an "outhouse." Once when Mrs. Myers went in to go to the bathroom, we heard screaming and saw her come running out of the outhouse with her dress up around her waist and her panties around her knees. There was a scorpion on the outhouse seat, and she thought she was going to get stung. It looked really funny seeing her running and screaming with her panties down. I had never seen her in less than a slip. Electricity got finally was ran to the property, Then Mr. Myers started framing in a big room, put plywood all around the outside, on the floor and then put a roof on it. A cook stove and refrigerator were purchased and set up in that room, so we didn't have to cook over an open fire anymore or try to keep food cold in coolers. We had to help with the construction every day, still living with the constant sexual, physical, and mental abuse until school started. We got to escape at least part of the day by going to school. I had never seen a school like that one was. I was in sixth grade and the school was long, each room was separate as I was used to, but each room had its own door facing outside. You had to go outside to go to your next class or even to use the bathroom. I was having trouble with school her and escaped to the bathroom whenever I could. When we would go back home the reality of our existence would hit again though and it would be back to work. On an evening when the Myers and all the kids were out, I was home by myself (I don't remember why) my brother Mark came in and he tried to get me to have sex with him. "Come on Kathy, you let him do it, why can't I?" I would not do it and he kept after me, knocked me to the ground, tried to take my clothes off. I was fighting him, but he managed to get my top up over my breasts and took one of my Breasts in his mouth. He sucked on it so hard while I was screaming and fighting him it really hurt. He finally stopped got up and left the house again all the while calling me names. I didn't tell on him though because I knew that Mr. Myers would kill him and again, I would be in trouble too so I just did the best I could to avoid him. Mrs. Myers seemed to have picked Mark as her favorite because Mr. Myers didn't like him and would be extremely sweet and kind to him while sending me dirty looks and Mr. Myers started treating me like I was his favorite, so Mark and I were pitted against each other. I always lost the fights with Mark though because he was four years older, taller and stronger than me. One of the times he was in trouble for some infraction by Mr. Myers, he came through the kitchen where I was standing and out of the blue, pushed me so hard, I fell between the stove and refrigerator. I had become afraid of and hated my own brother.

We would all go driving around and Mr. Myers would stop along the road where there were irrigation ditches to let us swim. Sometimes the dogs got to go too. One of the times we were swimming, the dogs jumped in, but they were too close to where the water is sucked down into the pipes to spray out in the fields. Mr. Myers was able to reach down and grab bumper and pull him out but no matter how much he tried he could not find the other dog, A man stopped by and told Mr. Myers we were trespassing and had to leave. Mr. Myers said she had been under the water way too long anyway and so had drowned and we left. We were not allowed to have friends over nor did we spend the night with any friends. There was a family that didn't live too far from where we did that we met, and they had a bunch of farm animals. They came over one day and asked the Myers if they would take the animals because their little boy had been attacked by a stray German Sheppard and it had bit off his nose. I had never seen anyone without a nose before. He looked like a skeleton but with skin on the rest of his face. He had all kinds of medical issues as well as a very strong fear of all animals because of it, so they were willing to give the animals to anyone that was willing to take them. The Myers agreed to take the chickens and a horse. Mr. Myers built a chicken house to put them in and a shed for the horse. We had to gather the eggs from the chicken house, they were kind of mean so you had to be careful not to get pecked when reaching into the nests for the eggs. The horse was way overweight and had not been ridden in a while but I thought that I was a good enough rider since I had ridden one in summer camp, so I faked being sick one day to stay out of school and later when "I felt better" I went out to ride him. We did not have a saddle, so you just rode bareback. I jumped up on his back and off we went. He let me ride him for a while without giving me any problems until I was far enough out that I could no longer see the house and all of a sudden, he bucked me off and took off running back to his barn. I landed right in the middle of a cactus patch! I tried to call him back, but he was long gone so I had to walk back home and then Mrs. Myers had to pick the cactus stickers out of my back. Mr. Myers started trying to teach Mrs. Myers how to drive because he said she had to because we were going to move again, and she would need to drive one of the vehicles. We left Arizona, again loaded all our belongings and headed for Pennsylvania with Mr. Myers driving the truck and Uhaul and Mrs. Myers driving the station wagon. Since Mrs. Myers had to drive always following behind Mr. Myers there was no protection from him for us at all. She could not see into the cab of the uhaul and it made it easy for him to move us to sit beside him and if we tried to get one of the other kids to ride with us, he stopped them by saying there was too much stuff in the seat so only one of us could go with him and he picked who it would be.

When I had to ride with him, he would make me sit beside him and on occasion he would slide his hand into my panties and fondle me or he would unzip his pants and take my hand and put it inside of the zipper to push against his penis. We would find roadside parks or would just pull up along a side ramp along the highway to spend the night. We didn't have much with us to eat one of those nights but a loaf of bread and cans of pork and beans. Mr. Myers showed us how to make pork and bean sandwiches and it was ok, we didn't mind, we were hungry and that was filling. When we were done there was still a partial can of beans left but none of us had wanted any more. Mr. Myers kept trying to get someone to eat them. Mr. Myers asked who wanted some candy and of course we all did, there is always room for candy, but it had been a trick, He said, "if we had room for candy then we had enough room for the rest of the beans" and he made us eat all of them.

The next morning when we woke up Mark was gone. He had run away in the middle of the night. None of us had seen or heard him get up and sneak away. The Myers were so mad; one of them had to get to a phone (we didn't have cell phones then) to call the police, wait for them to show up and make out a report and put out a missing persons bulletin. We waited around most of the day listening to Mr. Myers rant and rave about all the travel time we were losing, and we just did the best we could to stay out of the way. The police kept checking in with the Myers to give them a progress reports, but no one could find Mark so the Myers decided to move on and they would contact the police along the way to see if there was any news of Mark. I never heard anything about Mark after that. None of us knew where he had gone or where he was living. We just knew that he had made his escape!

We arrived in a small town called Bradford Pennsylvania and moved into a house out in the country. It was an older, two story house, but big enough for three adults and seven children. There was a large room that the Myers used for a bedroom and another large room that Ginger and Karen shared. The rest of us were upstairs, Linda got the biggest room, Brandy and Amy shared a room as well as Jason and Doug. There was a tiny room right off the top of the stairs that I think was previously a closet of some sort that I took as my room. It had one window and it was just big enough to fit a small cot and dresser into. I had never had a room to myself and was not too excited about it but was not given a choice. You had to go outside to get to the storm shelter and lift up double doors to get to it. There was a garage that sat separate from the house and a large double row of pine trees, from the garage to the backyard and then across the backyard, behind that was a forest. Our nearest neighbor was a mile away and the schools we attended were a fortyfive minute ride by school bus. I was in junior high now and liked my new school and the kids that we rode the bus with. I got along with my classmates, they called me tumbleweed as I was starting to come into my own, thinning out, getting taller and developing a womanly shape. I had a boyfriend at school "Steve " and my best friend was Teresa (she was one of the kids that lived a mile away) and we would walk to each other's house to hang out. I tried to go to her house as much as I was allowed. Her family owned and operated their own sawmill. We were not allowed to go anywhere near the mill or bunk houses that their help stayed in, but they had a large amount of property that they ran cattle on too and in one of the pastures was an old delivery van that Teresa and I used as our place to hang out and talk. During the winter the country kids would all meet at one of the local ponds, build a bonfire and we would all go ice skating. I had never ice skated until then and I loved it and went every chance I got.

Mr. Myers still was touching and having sex with me and I still did everything I could to avoid him. With me having a room to myself this became very difficult, so I started crawling under my bed with a pillow and one blanket, putting my back up against the wall even though I was afraid of spiders and tried to sleep under there. Sometimes I was allowed to sleep with Brandy and Amy but there wasn't enough room for three of us and Amy would end up in bed with Linda, so we weren't allowed to do that very often.

One night he entered my bedroom again picked me up out of my bed and carried me downstairs to the living room. He said, "I am going to teach you what it feels like to be a real woman." He proceeded to take off my pajamas and panties, opened my legs and put his mouth to my private parts. I squirmed trying to get away from him, tried to close my legs but he used his weight to hold me down. He ran his tongue up and down my slit and then concentrated on the button of my private. It did start to feel different than it ever had, my muscles tightened against my will, my body seemed to burst into a million pieces then it started becoming painful and I was again fighting him trying to get him to stop. The noise from my struggles must have awoken Mrs. Myers and she came down the stairs to find out what was going on. She started calling me a slut, yelling and screaming at me. We were in the archway of the kitchen and the living room on the floor. Mr. Myers jumped up, trying to calm her down. I don't remember what he was saying, only that Mrs. Myers had grabbed a butcher knife from the kitchen and was coming at me with it. Mr. Myers stepped between us and was keeping each of us on the opposite sides of him. You whore! she screamed at me and would lung at me with the butcher knife again but never seemed to get me. Ill teach you, you hussy, acting like I was the one raping him!

She never once tried to use that knife on him, all her concentration was on killing me and I wanted her to. So bad! I was ready to die and was fighting as hard as I could against Mr. Myers, to get to her so she could kill me. I wasn't afraid of the knife entering my body, all I could think of was that it would end the torture that I constantly lived with. It was not to be though; he got the knife away from her and she ended up crying and saying she was sorry that she didn't really want to kill me. Everything was ignored and life went on as it always had, like nothing had ever happened except now my life was even more miserable though as it seemed I could do nothing right in Mrs. Myers eyes. Everything I did was picked apart, not clean enough, not folded well enough, room not cleaned enough. She would dump everything out of my drawers and flip my bed over. Earning more slaps and hits, being yelled at and called names more frequently than ever by her. She would only give me a certain amount of time to clean the mess up or expect a beating. All of the kids knew I was in trouble and avoided me or were mean towards me because Mrs. Myers was mad at me.

Summer came and school was let out. I didn't get to see my boyfreind anymore. We tried to write but he ended breaking up with me. Now that we had met the neighbor kids and the kids we rode on the bus with, some of them started coming over during the summer. One of the boy's that came over was named Frank, He was very quiet and not very good looking, but he liked me and asked me to go steady with him. I wanted to fit in with the other girls so I said yes. He didn't come over real often though and I really didn't like him that way but just as a friend. I broke up with him. One of Karen's friends (Diana) had a brother that could drive. He took his sister, Karen and I with him to the lake for the day. He drove a jeep and had the top off on the ride there. It was so much fun to have the breeze blow through my hair and to feel so free. We all went swimming when we got there and most of us were good swimmers so had no life jackets on. Diana did not know how to swim but wanted to be out in the deep water with us, so she took a large beach ball to hold in front of herself and used that as her floatation device. She kicked her way out to us and all of a sudden, she lost her grip on the beach ball and went under the water. Panicking she grabbed me since I was the closest and tried to use me to get her head above water. She was literally trying to climb up my body and pushing me under the water. I was drowning and trying to get Diana off of me. No one seemed to realize what was happening so no one was helping either of us. I tried to hit her and knock her off at the same time I was trying to swim to shore. I finally got where I could stand up when others realized she was in trouble and came to help her to shore. I was coughing, trying to catch my breath and went on up to the beach. Diana was crying and telling me she was so sorry but had panicked when she lost the ball and all she could do was grab on to me.

Mr. Myers decided that we needed to get rid of the doors to the storm shelter and dig it out so you could walk into it from outside the house. He ripped the double doors off, and we started digging, by hand again of course, making a gradual slope until it was deep enough to put a regular size entrance door. You could also reach the storm shelter by going through the house and down the stairs, but it was just a hole dug out of the dirt and had spiders and creepy crawly things down there so none of us kids ever wanted to go down there. Again, we were made to help with any and all projects that he came up with and survive the physical and sexual abuse. One of the times I was required to help him he took my arm and drug me behind the row of pine trees, pulled down my pants and made me bend over. He took his penis and pushed it into and out of my vagina until he was ready to ejaculate, pulled his penis out of my vagina and spilt his seed on the ground, then told me to pull my pants back up and get back to work. The trees were thick and kept anyone from seeing behind them. He would come to my room on most nights and have sex with me. I would lay there like a mummy, unmoving, and tried to escape by leaving my body, ignoring him the best I could. In a box of junk, I found a lock, the kind that the bolt slides through. I took it and put it on the inside of my door so I could lock him out. He came to my room and could not get the door open, I heard him rattle the door and call my name in a low voice. I laid real still and he eventually went away. The next day he called me to come help him work on something in the garage. When I got out there, he asked me what I meant by locking my door. I was never to lock him out and I needed to remove the lock. He then striped my clothes off and raped with me right there in the garage. Ginger and Karen let me stay in their room with them one night and we were just sitting there talking when I heard a soft tapping. Ginger got up and went over to the window and slid it open. There was a couple of guys standing there and the girls started whispering back and forth with them. They had to be quiet because we didn't want to get caught. I was to be the lookout and let them know if anyone was coming so they didn't have to worry and could visit with their boyfriends. I didn't mind because this was the first time, they had included me in on something they were doing. They talked and kissed through the window for a long time then shut the window when the guys left, and we all went to bed.

Ginger and Karen decided that I could be trusted and started involving me more in their evening escapades. Mr. Myers had nailed the door to the basement shut so no one would sneak out at night, but he didn't think about the window. Each of us would very quietly crawl out the window and sprint across the back yard behind the pine trees and into the woods at the back of the house. We kept going until we came upon a bonfire and people would be standing around drinking beer. Ginger and Karen's boyfriends were there, and they would pair off and disappear. I would sit at the campfire and talk to everyone around but did not drink any beer or alcohole.

Another night, we walked to the Hervantines' house and went out to the bunkhouses the mill workers used. They met with their boyfriends there, disappearing into the bunkhouse for a while. It was great fun being included in all the scheming so they could see their boyfriends. Gingers' boyfriend was my old boyfriend, that I had broken up with the summer before, but his looks had completely changed, his acne was cleared up "Previously it had been really bad" and his body was muscled up. I was sorry I had broken up with him now and I was a little jealous of Ginger being with him. We were in Ginger and Karen's room again waiting for the guys to show up, watching to make sure we would not get caught when the guys tapped on the window this time though Mr. Myers came out from around the corner of the house and started yelling at the guys to get off his property. He was chasing them and yelling that he was going to call the police on them. The guys scattered in all directions running to get away from him. Mr. Myers then came into the bedroom with a hammer and nails and nailed the window shut. He came at all three of us girls with his leather belt then calling us whores and swinging the belt at us, hitting us all over our bodies, not caring where the belt landed, whether it was our hind end or our faces. Ginger just looked at him and refused to cry or shed a tear when he hit her, so he stopped hitting us, told us we were all grounded and left the room. He never whipped Ginger ever again because he did not get a reaction from her and she told us if we wouldn't cry or show that he was causing us pain that he would stop hitting us too. Not long after that incident we were packed up overnight and moving again. There was no warning that we were moving, we were literally packed and on the move within one night. I was able to sneak a call to Teresa and Lorl to tell them goodbye and get their mailing addresses so I could write to them.

This time we moved to Ogden Utah, where Mr. Myers took us to see an older Mexican man and introduced us to him as his dad. Mr.

Myers was not Mexican so it didn't make sense but who cared. Grandpa was nice, he made us homemade tortillas with potatoes and egg for breakfast and was always ready with a good hug and kiss when we saw him. I was in the eigth grade now. The last year of junior high. I ignored my home life for the most part, blocked out the visits and attacks from Mr. Myers. Half of my life was lived hidden inside of myself, I would disappear into myself and the only thing that existed was when I was in school. I had a boyfriend, at school that I really liked but Mr. Myers found out he was black and made me break up with him. The house we moved into had a big heater that stood on the floor about midthigh in high and 6 feet in length along one of the walls in the bedroom Karen and I shared. The heater would get supper hot to the touch and would burn you if you weren't careful. Karen and I were messing around one evening and playing tag with bumper, he liked to chase you around the house. We were laughing and running from him (I was wearing a teeshirt and shorts for my pajamas) when I ran right up alongside of the heater, you could hear my flesh sizzling the whole length of the heater and some skin was left on it. I tightly grabbed my thigh around the burn and Karen ran to get Mrs. Myers to come help me. It was a third degree burn and extremely painful. I was not allowed to go to school. Mrs. Myers and Linda had gotten their first jobs at a cafeteria at one of the colleges and was gone a portion of every day. Mrs. Myers, often brought left over food home which was helpful since Mr. Myers stayed at home now and financially things were tight. After everyone had left for school or work the next day Mr. Myers came into my room to check on my burn and apply the salve. After he was done applying it, and putting on a new bandage, he started touching my breasts, removing my clothes and talking to me, "my poor baby girl is hurt, let daddy make it all better." He touched my private, kissed and suckled at my breasts and then undressed himself, got on top of me, spread my legs, and entered his shaft into my vagina. I was unble to fight with the burn on my leg being so sever. He moved up and down, pushing into my vagina and then with drawing, almost pulling it all the way out and then would plunge it back into me, talking to me the whole time saying how much he loved me, how tight I was and how good I made him feel. He took his time moving in and out of me at a slow pace. Linda worked with Mrs. Myers at the college so there was no one there to help protect me and he knew he had all the time he wanted. I just disappeared into myself and was absent the whole time he was getting his kicks.

I finally healed enough to be able to wear a bandage over my burn and was able to return to school. I noticed a letter on the table one morning as I was leaving for school, it was from my sister Sandy and had her return address on it, so I stole it, an envelope and a stamp. I wrote to Sandy, telling her of all the sexual attacks and physical abuse I was living through, sealed, addressed and put the stamp on it, then took it to the front office and ask them if they could send it out for me. They saw it was already stamped so they took it and put it in with the outgoing mail. I did not get a letter back from her but some strange man I had never seen before came to my school and I was sent to the principal's office to visit with him. He introduced himself, said he was a private investigator and asked me all kinds of questions about my life with the Myers but refused to tell me who sent him. II asked over and over who had sent him but he refused to tell we and I was afraid that the Myers were the ones that had sent him, so I lied to him, told him I didn't know what he was talking about and that nothing bad was going on at my house. I had to be convincing because the Myers had tricked us before to see if wc would tell anyone and I was afraid that is what was going on and I must have done a good job because he left. Ginger was having a great school year, taking sewing lessons, getting good grades, and had decided to join the army. Ginger liked to talk to Karen and I at night about what Mr. Myers did to us and how it felt, where and how he touched us and if it felt good, did we like it? She seemed to almost get excited by talking about it, but it made us uncomfortable, so we tried to avoid those talks as much as possible. Now that Ginger was older and had made plans for her future she was allowed to do as she pleased for the most part. All the Myers talked about was how great Ginger was and how she would be their first child to graduate and how wonderful she was going to be in the army making all that money.

Karen and I were now allowed to wear makeup and shave our legs and armpits. We still had to wear dresses or skirts. We took great care every morning, fixing our hair, putting on makeup just so, picking out the perfect outfit. Karen had a tight yellow and black button up skirt that I loved and when she outgrew it, I got it. It had a real high waist band that made you look thin and was short enough to show a little thigh. The boys started to take notice of me after I wore that skirt, I was popular, and they flirted with me and I liked it. Karen and I wore skirts as often as we could because after we left the house it was easy to roll them up and make short skirts out of them, but you had to remember to unroll them back down to knee length before you got off the bus! I got caught one day when I came home and forgot to unroll the waistband and ended up getting a whipping with the belt and grounded. While in class one day "would Kathy Myers please report to the principal's office" came over the speaker loudly. The kids were teasing me saying oh you're in trouble now and what did you do? I didn't know why I was being called down to the office again but got up and went. As I was walking down the stairs, I looked down the hall and could see a couple of people standing with the principal and the same detective that I had talked to earlier at the other end. I couldn't tell who it was until I got a little closer and then I realized it was my sister Sandy and her husband Allen! Screaming her name, I ran toward her and slammed into her hugging, crying, and laughing with them both. We then went into the office to talk and she said that they were the ones that had hired the private detective and when he reported back that she was crazy there was nothing going on, she knew she had to come herself because she understood the fear that had kept me quiet. We went into the office and the detective ask me the same questions but this time my answers were honest, and I was able to let him know what had been going on. Leaving the school, we drove to Karen's school, had her called from class and we went to the detective's office from there. You will be very uncomfortable with all the questions I will have to ask you and it will seem like I am being hard on you but I have to make sure I have all the facts.

The cross examiner will be more direct and mean, try to trip you up to show you are lying and the Myers are innocent of all your accusations. With both of you getting on the stand it will make our case stronger and make it harder for him to do that. I had to give a detail, by detail description on where he touched me, how he touched me, what he touched me with and how he did it. That was so, so tough for a twelveyear-old girl, to tell a man and a group of people you had not ever met in your life, but I wanted it to end so I sucked it up and gave them every detail and every touch description I could.

Karen wouldn't hardly answer ay questions from either lawyer, she was terribly embarrassed and just kept crying. They called it a day when protective services came to say they had found us a home that was willing to take us in and that we needed to be going. We wanted to stay with Sandy and Allen, but they said we couldn't do that, but she would see us again tomorrow when we went back in for more questioning to get ready to go to court. The couple that took us in were fairly young. They were a nice and it was only to be a short term, "protective custody" basically to hide us out where the Myers wouldn't be able to find us. They had a small home, but it was nice and very homey looking. Karen and I got to share a room with bunkbeds in it and at first, we both wanted the top bunk so we decided we would take turns sleeping up there. After the first night neither of us wanted anything to do with the top bunk because the heat all rose to the top of the room and you got so hot you couldn't sleep. The room was set up for children much younger than Karen and I were. They had pets and toys in the yard, but we were too old for most of the toys. We felt out of place there and were not allowed to leave the yard, as if we were babies! We met with the lawyer to go over our testimonies. The questions he asked were so personal, the way he phrased them was making it sound like we were the ones at fault for what Mr. Myers did and when we acted upset by this type of questioning, he explained that he wanted us to know how the Defending lawyer would question us so we would not get rattled by him. It was hard and embarrassing to answer such personal questions; but I knew that I had to do it to get it to stop. Every Friday evening our foster parents would take us out to eat at a little hamburger joint, after a day spent at the lawyer's office. The hamburgers were as large as a dinner plate and you got a huge number of fries with it.

Most of the time it was a waste of their money though because neither, Karen, nor I had much of an appetite, but we did appreciate their efforts. Court day finally arrived and it was as bad as they told us it would be. When we entered the courthouse, the first people we saw was Mr. and Mrs. Myers in the hall and both of them just stood there staring at us with accusing looks. It was amazing that even after all the abuse that we had put up with it still hurt to have Mrs. Myers look at me with that hate filled accusing look.

Especially with knowing how he had abused her. Like I was the one that had caused all this trouble. It shook us up pretty bad and our lawyer quickly led us into a room where he could shut the door and tried to calm us down. I was called to the witness stand first. They had me go up in front of the room and step up to a small platform with a chair, raise my right hand and place my left hand on the bible, "do you swear to tell the whole truth and nothing but the truth so help you God" they asked me and I replied "yes."

They then told me I could sit down, and my lawyer approached the front where I was sitting and ask me "if I had been sexually and physically abused and if so, was the person or persons that committed those acts in the room? And could I point them out?" I said "yes" and pointed to the Myers. In my eyes and thoughts, it was only Mr. Myers that was the abuser, I still loved Mrs. Myers and it hurt terribly that she would stay by Mr. Myers side even though she knew that he had been abusing us. They ask me to tell them dates and times that Mr. Myers touched me inappropriately, how he touched me, where he touched me and what he touched me with. It was horrible and self degrading sitting there trying to describe, in detail all the times that I had been molested, raped and beaten. There weren't too many people allowed into the courtroom and most of them were men. There was the Myers, sitting there with their lawyer glaring at me with such hate. The Myers attorney did exactly what our Lawyer said he would by trying to make it look like I was lying, making stories up as a way to get back at the Myers for some wrong I felt they had done to me. I was finally able to get down from the witness stand and then Karen was called in. Karen started crying the minute she walked into the courtroom and saw how the Myers were glaring at her. Our lawyer quietly told her "not to look at them and try not to let them get to her" but it did no good. She kept crying and would not answer either of the lawyer's questions, so they only had my testimony to go by.

They adjourned and we were allowed to go back to the room we were previously in to wait for a verdict. We were in the room for about fortyfive minutes when someone came to the door and said they had a verdict and we needed to come back into the courtroom. The judge told us that we had a choice, "they were a "family" oriented state and believed in keeping the family together whenever possible so we could go back and live with the Myers, with Mr. and Mrs. Myers going to parenting classes and the court would keep an eye on them or we could become awards of the court and stay in foster care until Allen got out of the Army and he and Sandy could get legal custody of us." I was so amazed that they would actually think we would ever choose to go back and live with the Myers, I was in shock! Once I got over the initial shock of his question, I had no problem telling them I never wanted to go back. It was so ordered that we would remain in foster care and that Mr. Myers would be required to send us the portion of his disability check that was ours. We only got one check for about sixty dollars each and never got another dime but at least I never had to see him again.

That was when I learned that we had never been adopted. I had been born to Roland Ray Chapman and Anita Lenard Chapman on September 15th 1959 in Newport Beach California so my legal last name was Chapman not Myers so from that time, I started using Chapman as my last name instead of Myers. Once our case in court was settled the social worker came and told us they had found a new foster home for us, the one we were in presently was a temporary shelter to keep us hidden until we were done testifying. We had very little to pack because the Myers refused to give us any of our clothes or belongings. We had the clothes on our backs and what few things the current foster parents had been able to get us and nothing more. The courts would not judge on Doug, out little brother because he was not accusing the Myers of sexual abuse and that would be another case all together. They said they would have to figure another way to get Doug out of the home but in the meantime Sandy and Allen had to leave. Allen was still in the army and his commanding officer had given him special leave to come and help Karen and I but now that we were safe and in state custody they had to go back to Germany and finish serving his enlistment time so they could come back and petition for custody of us. It was very hard to say goodbye and watch them leave, the last familiar person other than Karen was leaving me and I felt so lost. We drove into a nice neighborhood where the houses were fairly close together, and they looked very fancy compared to what we were used to. The lawns were green and lush, mowed, and trimmed to perfection.

When our Social worker pulled up in front of one of those houses, we could not believe it! We were going to live in that beautiful house? A lady by the name of Sharon was there to greet us, took us into the back of the house that served as an office for the ceramic shop they had in the garage. Sharon was going to be our new foster mother. She had short brown hair, wore glasses and was a very small woman but had a very authoritive personality, we were to find out. After the social worker left, Sharon showed Karen and I around and it was nice. We had our own bedroom, and they had an indoor pool that we could swim in, we could make ceramics, or just hang out with the neighbor kids. When Larry came home from work, Sharon introduced him as our foster dad and said that he worked for the railroad. Sharon took Karen and I shopping and got us both some clothes, makeup and personal items. They had a camper that fit over a pickup truck that we would all load up into and go camping different places. It was very crowded but Sharon and Larry always included Karen and I with their kids in everything they did. We were never left out because Sharon said they had committed to being our parents and that was how they were going to treat us. None of us kids seemed to mind that it was crowded, in fact I think we all had a great time and met some very interesting people in our travels. Karen and I even got to go to a summer camp for girls. I met up with a couple girls there that were always pulling one stunt or another. I thought it was funny and they accepted me and included me in the stuff they did. I felt accepted and maybe a little bad, for all our stunts, but for the first time in my life not afraid. The last day of camp was rather special. There were ceremonies and awards given out but the one that stood out the most to me was called the rose ceremony. All the campers would vote on who they thought the nicest person was all week and they were given a dozen roses and a crown. I didn't know they did that, but it was very touched by it. Sharon and Larry eventually bought a motor home and sold the truck and camper. Now that was traveling in style! Marcia, Karen and I would make signs with notebooks and magic marker saying hi or smile and hold them up for people in the vehicles beside us to read. It seems silly now, but we had fun with it. The summer seemed to go by so fast! Sharon had never had her ears pierced and was always wearing the clipon type that pinched your ears. When she saw that ours were pierced and we told her it really didn't hurt that much to get them pierced, she decided to get hers done too, then Marcia and Jeanie got to get theirs pierced too. She really loved not having to wear those clipon earrings anymore! Karen was enrolled into Ogden High, and I was enrolled into middle school. Several of the kids on my block went to the same school and attended the Morman church Sharon and Larry belonged to so I had met several of the kids before I started school. One of the girls in my class "Cathy" knew the Allen's because her mom worked for them at the ceramic shop and they attended the same church, showed me around school, where my classes were and introduced me to some of the kids. We became very good friends and started hanging out quite a bit with another friend named Kori. Cathy was tall, thin, blond, and bold, KorI was short, tiny, long dark brown hair and fun to be around.

We became the three musketeers, eating lunch together at school, going over to each, others houses' after school, skipping school, (we wrote excuse notes for each other) and thumbing rides out to the lake, spending the whole day laying in the sun and swimming then having to thumb our way back home trying to make it close to the time we should be getting home from school. I am amazed but I never did get busted for doing that. We were always able to catch a ride and made it back in time. We were absolutely crazy but for the first time in my life, I was not afraid, I felt free and that I could make my own choices. Summer came and we had chores we had to do just like a normal family. We took turns washing the dishes, folding clothes and sometimes helping out in the ceramic shop. Sharon and Larry took us on quite a few vacations and or camping trips that we all always enjoyed. I wanted to get a job during the summer so I could have my own spending money and buy my own school clothes I found a job as a car hop in no time, even though I wasn't actually old enough to work, the owner said I looked like I was old enough and I looked him right in the eye and was honest, so he felt good about hiring me. Sharon and Larry were fine with that and made sure that I got to my job and got picked up once my shift was over. Sharon didn't make me do many of the chores once I got a job because I was working and not just hanging out at the house. I didn't make a lot of money, but I worked hard, was polite to my customers and I noticed that some of the people I had waited on would come back and always park in the area I was working.

They tipped me well and nicknamed me bubble gum. One day at work the wind was blowing super hard and it was raining on and off. When I was giving change to a customer a twentydollar bill blew out of my pouch. Another customer picked it up but refused to give it back to me. I knew that I would have to make up that twenty dollars out of my own pocket, so I tried very hard to get him to give it back to me, even getting my boss involved with trying to get him to give it back. The customer refused to give it to me unless I could tell him what numbers were on the bill, which of course I could not do. Normally, my boss would have us make up any money we were short, but because he knew what had happened, he didn't make me put it back. I saved my money, putting it in a piggy bank that Sharon had given me and when it was time to get ready to go back to school, I bought my own clothes with the money I had saved. Karen had gotten a job that summer too, but it didn't last very long so she ended up staying home. She was not very happy about that because she is a year older than I am and complained about feeling like I was allowed much more freedom than she was.

Which was true. I was allowed more freedom than she was, but Sharon said it was because I acted more mature and held down a job.

That was the summer I met Mark, Cathy's older brother. Mark was several years older than me and was kind of a bad boy. He was in his twenties, had long blond hair, about shoulder length, blue eyes and rode a motorcycle and he liked me! I went riding with him on the bike one day and that was when we decided that we really liked each other and wanted to spend more time together but Sharon and Larry didn't approve of him, one because of the bad boy image and two he was too old for me, so we snuck around to see each other with the help of Cathy of course. The time we could spend together was very limited because of the restrictions, he had to work, I had to go to school. He stayed home from work one day (he still lived with his parents) and I skipped school. With everyone gone to work or school, we had his house all to ourselves for the day, we stayed in his room and just talked, kissed, hugged and slept all day long. We would wake up, talk more, then sleep again knowing that Cathy would come home from school and make sure that I headed home so no one would catch us. Even Cathy could not believe all we did was sleep but Mark told her that after everything I had been through, that was the last thing he would do to me. He did not want to use me and that I meant more to him than that. Eventually Sharon and Larry did find out about Mark, because all us girls were sleeping out on the patio one night and I snuck out after everyone was asleep to see him and go riding on the motorcycle. Sharon decided to check on us and I was not there. They were waiting up for me when I got home. They stepped in to put a stop to our seeing each other. They met me in the living room the next morning and told me that I was going to have to go to a different foster home because I was a minor and Mark an adult and they could not allow us to see each other. I begged and promised that I would not see Mark anymore but did not want to go to another home so after several long conversations and tears I was allowed to stay. I don't know what was said to Mark, he left home, and I did not ever see him again. I guess Sharon figured out that I had a bit of a chip on my shoulder, and she took just me with her one day. There was a hospital where we went to the children's ward and there were so many children in hospital beds that were hurt so much more than I had ever been hurt, physically at least. I saw children with broken bones and burns all over their bodies that their parents had done to them and it made me realize even though I had been horribly abused, those children had it much worse than I did and that I needed to quit feeling so sorry for myself and stop being such a mean person.

We got to go to the girl's camp again not too long after they caught me out with Mark. When I arrived, I noticed the two friends I had made last year weren't there. That was actually okay with me because I had decided that I liked the idea of winning the rose ceremony. I wanted to be that girl that everyone liked and that got the roses and a crown at the end of the week. I worked very hard to be that person that helped everyone and was so nice but didn't win the ceremony. I did however win because that is the kind of person I decided I wanted to be all the time. I felt better being that kind and helpful person. Several months later I started dating Kent with the approval of Sharon and Larry. Kent was a college student and lived with his parents across the street from Sharon and Larry, came from a good family, an only child and had never had a girlfriend. He was several years older than me and I couldn't believe that he liked me! Both of Kent's parents were Japanees.

They did not approve of me, they wanted a Japanees daughter in law and did not encourage our relationship at all. They had many arguments with Kent about me, but Kent kept going out with me anyway. I really thought I was in love with Kent and will always have a place in my heart for that first real love. He took me to a concert once but for the most part, we just hung out together. Kent bought me a ring, but it was a little large and one day, when we were wrestling around and the ring flew off my finger. We tried to find it but never could. Kent and I never went beyond kissing, hugging or gentle petting but the attention and the way he treated me will always remain with me.

I cried my eyes out when Sharon and Larry told us that Allen and Sandy, my brother in law, and sister had come back to the states and petitioned the courts for custody of Karen and I and it had been granted. We had to pack our belongings and the government paid to fly us to Kansas to live with Allen and Sandy. Kent and I did not want to be separated, we both cried and held each other, promised that we would write every day and as soon as I was old enough, I would move back to Utah to be with him. The flight might have been exciting if I had been able to stop crying long enough to notice. My heart was breaking, and I did not want my life to change. I liked it just as it was, where it was and though I loved Sandy, I did not want to live in Kansas because Kent was not there.

Allen and Sandy picked us up from the airport in Kansas City then drove back to Ottawa Kansas where they had rented an older house with enough rooms for all of us. It was just something temporary until they could buy a house in Pomona, a town about ten miles west of Ottawa. We still had to start school in Ottawa. Karen and I did not fit in very well. Most of the kids had lived and went to school together their whole lives and we were outsiders. I didn't like the school, didn't have any friends and I missed Kent something terrible. Allen and Sandy bought their house in Pamona Kansas, so we packed up and moved again, this time the house was brand new though and it was nice. Unfortunately, life does not work out the way we plan most of the time. Kent and I did write back and forth but as time went on it was less and less often, and the following summer when I got to go back for a few weeks to visit, Kent was not the same person I had left behind and I am sure I had changed too. Kent was hanging out with a guy that lived down the street from him and he wasn't a very good person. He was into drugs and I noticed that Kent just didn't act like the same person. The separation it seemed had changed us both and the feelings weren't the same, my first true love was not the same person that he used to be.

Karen and I started going to Pamona high. It was a small town and a small school so everyone there had pretty much grown up together and had went to the same schools. Fortunatly, we were welcomed by almost everyone and seemed to fit right in with our class mates. I had a couple of boyfriend through my freshman year. One of my boy friends was a senior and very popular. He was dating a friend of mine but broke up with her because she cut off her long hair. We went out for a while. Around Christmas time, we went out and were exchanging our Christmas gifts to each other. I had bought him a nice men's bracelet engraved with our names and he gave me a nice watch. Then he decided we needed to have a talk about our relationship. He told me I had to have sex with him to be his girlfriend. I was so angry that he said that, I broke up with him. I had had enough of being forced to have sex and no one was going to do that to me again!

I had made a good friend by the name of Bev. I had been out to her house and met her parents and they liked me. Bev wasn't allowed to date unless I went with her, but I had been on many blind dates that she had set up for me through the guy she was dating, and it was always the same story. They were way too old and gross for me. My dates thought that they were going to get lucky and that was the only reason they agreed to go on the date. It became so bad that I told her no more blind dates! During my break from the blind dates, I became friends with Rodney through a girl at school and he asked me out. He was tall, blond, athletic and handsome so of course I said yes. We dated for a while and I was invited to his house for dinner with his family. His brother, Jeff was in my class and I really liked him too but only as a friend. We went to Rodney's house several times for dinner, out on dates to the movies and to the school dances together. Rodney and I had been going steady for a while when we decided to "go all the way". Everything was great until I thought I was pregnant. Rodney wanted to get married but said that we would do it like his parents did. He would go on to college while I got a job and took care of the baby. Just listening to him scared me because that is exactly what his mother did. She dropped out of school, got a job and took care of the babies and once his dad graduated college, he left her flat for someone else because she wasn't smart enough for him, leaving her to take care of the boys. I didn't want any part of that. I told him it was a false alarm and then broke up with him, telling him I wasn't ready for that kind of responsibility.

Bev was begging me to go on a blind date again because she really wanted to go out with some guy she had met and her parents wouldn't let her go unless she double dated. I told her no way that we had already done that, but she said it would be different this time. She was going to set me up with her cousin and he was really nice and good looking too. She showed me a picture and he was very handsome so I finally gave in and said I would go. Of course, when I spent the night at Bev's house, I didn't tell my sister that I would be going out on a date. As far as she knew, I was just spending the night with my friend. I rode the bus to Bev's house after school and we ate supper with her family and then went to Bev's room to get ready for our dates. We were putting the final touches on our makeup when Bev's brother knocked on the door and said our dates were there to pick us up. We quickly finished and went out to the living room where they were waiting for us but my date was not there. Instead, there was a blond guy, about my height, with blue eyes standing there with Bev's date and they were explaining that my date had gotten grounded so Arnold (that was his name) was filling in for him.

We went on our date and I liked Arnold. He was very nice, kind of shy but not too bad. He was good looking and had a great smile and a good sense of humor. I sat on my side of the car and he asked me if

I was afraid that he would bite me. Then told me to scoot over beside him. We hit it off right away and it was the best blind date I had ever been on. It was also to be the last blind date I would ever go on. I don't know why, but I knew almost right away that he was going to be the man that I would marry. We went out almost every weekend after that and I eventually gave in and had sex with Arnold just a couple of weeks later. I just felt like what am I saving myself for? My virginity had been stolen long ago and I really, really liked Arnold. We went to Worlds of Fun on one of our dates with Bev and her date. At the time, I thought that I might be pregnant (with Rodney's baby) but didn't know for sure. I told Arnold that there was a possibility and he said that we would worry about that if and when we knew for sure. Being a kid, I didn't even think about what the rides would do if I was. Right after we got off one of the rollercoaster rides, I got my period, so I thought everything was going to be okay, but it wasn't. I came home from school the next week and when I walked into the house Sandy was making hamburger helper for supper and the smell from it hit me like a sledgehammer! I was instantly sick to my stomach and ran for the bathroom and lost everything that was in my stomach. Sandy knew at that moment that I was pregnant and took me to the doctor. She said that I had to have an abortion but when I saw the doctor, he said that no one, not even my sister could force me to abort my baby. It was completely my choice and sent me home to think about it. Arnold and I had already discussed getting married, but we were going to wait for me to graduate school. When I called him to tell him I was pregnant and that we needed to decide what we were going to do, he said that we were going to get married. It was just going to be a little earlier than we had planned. I told him no, I didn't want to marry him just because I was pregnant. That we didn't even know if it was his baby or Rodney's. I wanted someone that was going to love me and marry me because they really wanted me. He said that he really did love me and really did want to get married and raise our family together. I finally agreed to marry him, but we still had to face his family. I had met Arnold's parents. They were very religious and wore clothing that reminded me of the Amish people. Having a meeting with them was not going to be easy. My sister and I went to his families' home to talk to them about my being pregnant and what we were going to do. They were very upset. Said Arnold was a black sheep and no good. They didn't say too much about me while I was sitting there but really got mad at Arnold because while they were calling him a black sheep, he kind of laughed. They told him that it wasn't anything to be laughing about. Arnold's family lived in another town that was about fortyfive minutes from my sister's house so trying to plan the wedding and get everything done since I had no car was very difficult. A couple from Arnold's parents, church (Don and Kathy) offered to let me stay with them until we got married. They were very kind and offered all kinds of help. I very much appreciated everything they did for Arnold and I. One of the member ladies helped me make my wedding dress and I made a shirt out of the same material for Arnold. I was so proud of my effort to make his shirt but when he went to put on his tie, the neckline was too small to button up. He was so happy that he couldn't button it because he had been trying to get out of wearing a tie all along. Arnold's best friend Paul agreed to be his best man and Bev was my bridesmaid. Paul's girlfriend and the time, and one of his cousin's girlfriends agreed to be the candle lighters. Another lady that lived in the community owned a flower shop and made all the flowers including my bouquet. A couple of Arnolds cousins made the wedding cake and also served and the reception. The wedding day came up very soon. We were married June 26th 1976 at the Danforth chapel on Kansas University grounds. I was sixteen years old and pregnant, and Arnold was nineteen. I knew only a couple of the people at my wedding. My sisters missed the wedding because they got lost trying to find the chapel. After being announced man and wife, we walked out of the chapel to the sound of whooping and hollering coming from a bus full of college students. We left the chapel to go out to a dairy farm that Arnold's best man and best friend's family lived. There were so many people that came to the wedding and reception that I didn't know but they were so kind and caring, trying to help us get a start on our life together.

Our first home was a very small one bedroom trailer that had a small area in the hall that we could fit a crib. It sat on the corner of a dairy farm. Arnold worked every day and I stayed home and tried to learn how to take care of a house and to cook. I was only sixteen years old, had no idea how to cook but Arnold's mom had three boys before she finally had a girl' so all the boys learned how to clean, cook and sew. Arnold showed me the basics and I took it from there. It felt like I had lost all my friends. They lived forty five miles away and were doing all the fun things you do in the summer and I was pregnant, didn't have a car or the gas money even if I did have a car. Arnold helped me learn how to put up and can food out of the garden to help with the cost of food. We couldn't afford much but were still very happy to have each other. Paul, Arnold's friend still came over to see him and I could tell he didn't like me much. He tried on several occasions to get Arnold to go out on me but thank God Arnold didn't do it. We both figured out that it wasn't really that Paul didn't like me but that he missed hanging out with Arnold like he used to. They grew up together, were the same age and did pretty much everything together until I came along. The pregnancy was normal, and I had just starting to get too big for my regular clothes. I was due January 17th 1976. Exactly one week after Arnold's birthday. In December, we decided to go on a short ride to get out of the house for a small time as I was stuck there most days while he was at work. When we got home, I was walking up the sidewalk to go into the house and slipped on the ice. I fell hard right onto my bottom. It felt like all my insides were going to fall out. Eventually,

Arnold was able to help me up and into the house where I laid down for a little while but not too long. We were going to Paul's family's house for dinner that night. During dinner and while helping with cleaning up from the dinner, I had a small lower back ache. Lois, Paul's mother noticed me rubbing it and said that I needed to sit down. They kept watching me and said that they thought I might be in the first stages of labor and that I may need to go see the doctor. I told them that I had an appointment the very next morning and I would let him know about the ache. I didn't sleep well that night as the ache in my lower back wouldn't go away. The next morning getting ready for my doctor's appointment I couldn't get my shoes on. My feet were so swollen, so decided that I would just wear my house slippers. I showed up at the doctors in a pale orange maternity dress and pink fluffy slippers! I am sure I looked hilarious! Once I got into the doctor's office, he took one look at me and told me to get my butt over to the hospital. That I was in labor and it was too early. I had just started wearing maternity clothes and was actually pretty small and just looking at me, it didn't look like I was anywhere near ready to give birth. I checked into the hospital, called Arnold and then they started giving me the shots to stop the contractions. I had to get a shot every hour and they hurt! When the nurse came in to give me another shot, I told her no, I could feel the baby coming. She told me not to be silly, that they had saw that I had fallen asleep so I couldn't still be having the contractions. I told her, "I felt ever one of them and I will not let you give me a shot until the doctor checks me out". She was angry but left to go get the doctor to check me. The doctor came in and said "what is this I hear about you not letting the nurse give you your shot?" I told him I felt the baby coming out and he said, "let me have a look" and the next thing he was saying is "get her into delivery now! She's crowning. On December 11th I gave birth to a squalling red faced ugly little girl. She looked all boney and blotchy and red. She had a whole lot of hair though. We named her Tessa Lynn and she became our world. When we arrived home from the hospital and walked into the trailer, I was so surprised! My two sisters, Sandy and Karen had brought a Christmas tree and decorations over and had it all set up! That was so sweet of them! We didn't have the money to get gifts for each other, so we set Tessa, in her carrier under the tree and took pictures of her. She was our Christmas that year. Once Tessa was born Arnold's parents seemed to accept me a little better and they loved being grandparents. They got Tessa as much as we were willing to let her go and when I was able to start working, they did the baby sitting. Kay, Arnold's sister still lived at home and she loved spending time with Tessa too. At times, I would get very upset with her because she would act like she was her mother. I had to work and did like that I didn't have to worry over who had her or if she was being taken care of. I worked very hard trying to develop a relationship with my mother and father inlaw, because I felt like I didn't have parents and that it would be wonderful if I could have that kind of relationship with them. Arnold was very good with Tessa and helped take care of her and played with her when he was home. We bought our first house in 1977 and had been attending the church AJ had grown up in. We made the decision to join the church and had the "uniforms" made. The men had to wear button up pants with suspenders and black hats. Keep their hair short and if they grew a beard, they were never allowed to cut it off. My uniform was a dress with a shawl and apron attached. You could wear short sleeves at home, but they had to be long sleeved if you went out anywhere. The dresses had to be long, down to your ankles. You couldn't own a television or radio. In fact, if your car had a radio, you had to take it out and remove the antenna. About the only entertainment that was allowed was to visit other members or go out to eat. I wanted AJ's family to accept me so badly that I thought that by becoming a member of their church it would fix all the problems and they would accept me as their daughter. It didn't help at all. I was still treated as an outsider from AJ's family. AJ's sister seemed to accept me and we hung out quite often. One day we were out hitting local garage sales and she made a statement to me that left me speechless. She said, "when she first me she thought I was really ugly but your personality makes up for it." I realized that no matter what I did, none of AJ's family was ever going to accept me and that I was not happy trying to live such a strict life. I told AJ that I just couldn't do it and dropped out of the church. He decided that if I wasn't going to be a member then he wasn't going to either and he dropped out too. I found out I was pregnant again, but AJ didn't want another child and wanted me to get an abortion. I just couldn't do that, and he made the statement at that time, "if I had this baby, he would make sure we had food and a roof over our heads, food to eat and clothes to wear but that was it." He "would not help with taking care of them. I went ahead with the pregnancy much to AJ's dismay. During the pregnancy, AJ ignored me most of the time and didn't help with Tessa at all. He said that I was unattractive and fat. Our sex life was pretty much nonexistent, because he didn't find me attractive. I was gross and fat, totally unattractive. This time I went to the other extreme and went over my due date. I was due the first part of July. When I went over the due date, they had me go to the hospital once every week and would put me into a light labor to check if the baby was getting enough oxygen and blood and as long as the baby was okay, they would not induce my labor to have it. I hated going in to do those tests because they made me vomit every time. The baby was stubborn and didn't make her entrance until August 25th. She was chubby, bald and very calm. The doctor looked at me after her birth and said "you have a month old baby there", I named her Mary Nichole. My sister Karen came to help me our right after Mary was born, bringing her son that was right between the girls in age. I appreciated the thought of her help but with three kids being there it wasn't making it too easy. One day when Arnold got home from work, he took Karen out for a motorcycle ride leaving me with the two kids and a newborn. They were gone for a long time and I got very angry and told Karen that I didn't need her help anymore and that she needed to go back home. I didn't believe that they had done anything but go for a joy ride, but she was supposed to be helping me, not leaving me with all the kids to watch. Arnold was true to his word and did not have much to do with either of the girls. He even stopped paying attention to me, unless he wanted to have sex. It seemed that was the only time I wasn't invisable. He would come home from work and it didn't seem to matter how hard I tried, and I did try everything I could think of, he would only notice the things that didn't get done in the house but not anything I worked so hard to get done. It seemed like he was always angry and nothing I did was ever good enough.

I decided to go to the high School and take the test to get my GED because I found that getting a job without a high school diploma was very difficult. Plus, I wanted to be able to say that I did graduate in 1978, the year I was supposed to. Not long after Mary was born AJ and I decided to move to Arizona where Sandy and her husband Allen and their children were living. I missed her terribly and they said there was work there and it stayed warm all the time.

We packed everything we could into a uhaul trailer and anything that we weren't able to take, we took over to AJ's parents. That was the first time I ever heard AJ's dad curse. He was carrying the TV antenna to put over in the metal pile and had it sticking up in the air while he was walking. It hit the overhead electric wire and gave him a really good shock. It was so funny to see his reaction and hear him cuss we couldn't help but laugh. When we arrived in Arizona, we stayed with Allen and Sandy for a couple of weeks while trying to get an apartment. Everyone loved Mary and gave her a lot of attention so when we moved into our own apartment, she was terribly fussy because she wasn't getting all the attention anymore. Arnold got a job there right away working for the same construction crew that Allen worked for. It was brutally hot out so the crews would start very early in the mornings and get off work about 2:00 pm. Sandy and Allen weren't getting along and ended up moving back to Kansas. After Sandy and Allen left, Arnold got offered a job hanging overhead doors from a door company. He had shown the pictures to one the bosses at a company that hung big commercial doors, of the doors he had hung while working for The Overhead Door Company in Kansas City. Arnold went to work for them. He traveled all the time and would be gone for weeks at a time. I was lonely with no family or friends and I didn't like being left with the kids all by myself. Mary was a tough kid to take care of. When she didn't get her way, she would cry so hard, she would make herself pass out. It scared me so bad I called the doctor. He had me bring her in to check her out but said there wasn't anything wrong with her. Just a bad temper and to keep a small glass of water in the refrigerator. If she started throwing a temper tantrum, get the glass of water and throw it in her face. It wouldn't hurt her other than making her a little wet but would make her catch her breath. It worked great! After she found out that didn't work anymore, she went through biting herself, pulling her own hair and repeatedly throwing herself on the floor. There were times while Arnold was gone that I didn't have any money to get groceries or gas. I would soak beans to cook so we would have something to eat. I didn't have a washing machine or dryer or the money to go to the laundry mat so I would kneel by the bathtub and wash our laundry by hand, wring it out and hang it over the back fence to dry. It was hard, back breaking work and killed my knees but at least our clothes were clean. That worked great until one day when I got up and went to get the clean clothes off my fence, I noticed that my laundry wasn't there. I ran outside and went around to the outside of the fence, but it wasn't there either. Someone had actually stolen our clothes and a couple of blankets that were drying out there. I would babysit for others to try and get some cash but many times they didn't have the money to pay either. I tried a telemarketing job but didn't make any money unless I got someone to buy something. I decided I needed a better job and signed at a dental school to become a dental assistant. Finding and affording childcare turned out to be impossible though so I was not able to complete the course.

Arnold never bought me any kind of gifts, not even for Christmas or my birthday. I always bought something even if it wasn't a big gift; it was at least something to show I cared and that I loved him. His excuse was that he wasn't raised that way and he just didn't think about it. I didn't and still don't buy that excuse though because I know where he worked gave him a bonus at Christmas time. It wasn't much, just a fiftydollar gift card and I mentioned to him that he could get the girls or me something for Christmas with it but instead, he gave me a dirty look and said that it was his gift from his work, and he was going to get something for himself. He bought a handheld football game and neither the girls, nor I were able to touch it. My feelings were hurt because he only thought of himself and the game, he bought cost more than the gift card and he thought nothing of paying out the extra money for it. He didn't get a thing for any of us, and I told him that he didn't have to spend a lot. A simple card or a flower, just something that let me know he thought about us would be good enough.

One day Arnold (AJ) called, (the short version of his name the guys that he worked with called him), I was extremely frustrated with the way things were going and how it seemed like his life was so carefree while I was struggling just to make sure our kids had something to eat. It seemed like he was enjoying life to the fullest, eating at fancy restaurants while I was struggling to get by with the girls. He talked about all the things he was doing and seeing and about the fantastic meals they went out to eat. He didn't really seem like he had a worry at all about what was happening with the girls and me. It seemed like we weren't a part of his life, more of a hindrance and he only called when it was convenient, or he was bored. Everything was about him and we were the last thing on his list. I don't know why but one day when he called and I listened to all the things he had been doing, I just felt like we were not an important part of his life so I decided to ask him what my middle name was, and he couldn't tell me. I then asked him how old I was. He couldn't even come close to my age either. It felt like something inside me broke that day. I knew everything about him, his age, his middle name, his likes and dislikes but he knew nothing about me. I had given him my all and he had nothing to give me. He had married me only because I was pregnant and had never truly loved me like I loved him. I told him we needed to talk when he came home and that I thought I wanted a divorce. I didn't want to stay married to someone that knew nothing about me. Not long after that I met a man that was very nice. He listened to me and we had long conversations. We did go on a couple of dates, but he was very honest with me and told me he was gay. I still liked him and enjoyed our talks. The funny thing about it was that he looked so much like AJ! I was drawn to him because he looked so much like him and he was a good listener on top of that.

When AJ came home, we had a long talk. Neither of us yelled or cursed at each other. I told him how I felt, and he said that he had been thinking about us too and that he did love me. He admitted that when he married me, he really wasn't in love with me but married me because of the pregnancy. It hurt to hear that because that was the very reason that I didn't want to get married in the first place, but he convinced me at the time, that wasn't the reason and that we had already planned on getting married eventually. He was crying and said that he didn't realize how much he had come to love me until I said I wanted a divorce. We talked for a long time and decided to pack everything up and move back to Kansas. To try to learn to love each other and to live as a family without him traveling all the time. It wasn't easy but I was still in love with my husband and wanted things to work out, so we moved into a trailer out in the country close to AJ's aunt and uncles house in Kansas. It wasn't a very nice trailer, but we knew it would be for just a short period of time. AJ's brother Roger had bought a trailer house from one of his cousins that was on about three acres of land and he decided to let us rent that from him. We both got jobs that let us be home in the evenings and worked on getting our marriage together. Unfortunately, he was still the same with the girls though and wouldn't take them anywhere or do anything with them. He would take my nephews fishing and do things with them, but the girls were never allowed to go unless I was there to take care of them.

One day Sandy called and said that Mark, our brother, had called her. He was living in Kansas City and wanted to meet up with us all. Sandy had just lost her youngest son Jason and there for a while I thought we had lost her too. She still had the older three children to take care of but was having a difficult time dealing with the loss of Josh. It changed her somehow and she got kind of wild. Going out all the time, dating a bunch of different guys and she got supper skinny. So skinny that she was scaring me! I always had plenty of space at my house so we decided to have everyone come to our house and that we would have a picnic. Sandy gave Mark our address and he showed up with a lady named Linda and three boys and a girl. Mark said Linda was his girlfriend and that the kids were hers. I noticed when Mark said to do something though, that they wasted no time jumping to do what he said. I still had a fear of Mark, but I liked Linda and the children. I couldn't understand what Linda saw in him but maybe he was good to her and the kids. We had a good visit and meal with Mark catching us up on all that they had been doing and where they had traveled to and then everyone went back home. We eventually bought some land, found a house that they were going to move out of an old housing community and paid for it and hired someone to move it onto some property we bought. It was one that had to be repaired. Basically, gutted and rebuilt but we knew AJ had the skills to remodel it and make it into a nice home for us. We got into an argument about the paint. I wanted to go with semigloss because I knew that would be easy to wash when needed, and he insisted that we go with flat paint. Later, we ended up having to go back and completely repaint with the semigloss because we found out that you can't wash the fingerprints or dirt off flat paint. We were getting along fairly well for the most part. I got a job and AJ was working too. With two children to take care of, I wasn't making enough money to make it worth my while. I was paying out more in childcare and gas than I was bringing in, so we made the decision for me to stay home with the girls and for AJ to make the money. I didn't have any money of my own because I stayed home so if I needed anything, I had to ask AJ for the money. He would only give me a little bit, like twenty dollars, and I had to try to get by with that. We planted a large garden and I processed as much of the food as I could. For Christmas AJ's mom and dad gave us meat to put in the freezer so we did not go hungry. I used what little money I could get from AJ and bought what I could for AJ and the girls for Christmas so they all had something under the tree Christmas morning. It wasn't much, some stuffed animals and a doll for each of the girls. I don't remember what I got for AJ, but they all had something to open. There was never anything under the tree for me. It hurt that he didn't think enough of me to even give me a Christmas present. I sat and watched them open their presents and took the pictures. I did my best not to show my hurt because I didn't want to ruin Christmas for the girls.

AJ's parents still had a great relationship with Tessa and liked to get her to come spend time with them. I had no problem with them taking her but once Mary got old enough, she started noticing that they never took her and she wanted to go too. When she asked to go, they would tell her no. It hurt me to see her feelings get hurt every time. I talked to AJ about it, and we decided that they either had to take both or take turns taking the girls so one wasn't always left out. When we talked to them about it, they said that both the girls were just too much to handle so we told them that was okay, but they needed to take turns with the girls, or they couldn't take either of them. They decided that if they couldn't just take Tessa, then they wouldn't take either of them so from that point on, they no longer had any kind of relationship with our daughters. Mark and Linda came to our Easter egg hunt/ picnic and I noticed that Linda's daughter, Teresa was pregnant. I got a really weird feeling when talking to her and to Linda about the pregnancy, but they were all saying the father was some guy at school. Teresa was giving them problems at home and they asked if she could come stay with us for a while. I really liked Teresa and felt that she needed help, so we said yes. Once Teresa moved in, I tried to question her about the father because I had a strong suspicion that Mark was the father and that he had molested her. She denied it and stuck to the story of the boy at school and eventually went back home to live with her family. When I first saw the baby, I knew I had been right. That baby was the picture of Mark. They were still trying to tell the same story, but we all knew better. The last I heard was through Sandy and she said that Teresa was pregnant again and that her and Mark were getting married and that he admitted that both of the children were his. We didn't see them again for several years. They just seemed to disappear which we knew Mark was good at. Four or five years later Mark contacted us again and invited us to Kansas City to visit Teresa and him. We went because I wanted to see Teresa and make sure the kids were okay. They were living in a small apartment and Daisy and Jack were both doing well. Daisy looked like Mark with the darker skin and Jack had Mark's features but Teresa's coloring. I could tell Teresa had put on a little weight and she seemed to tear up easily. The guys ran to the store and left us with the children and during the time they were gone Teresa informed me that she had just given birth to a little boy. Mark had sold him and his oneyear–old brother to some lady and when Teresa had tried to stop him he beat her. She was terrified of him and had been so beaten down that she wouldn't let me help her. I knew how mean Mark could be and so I didn't say anything to AJ about it until we were on our way home. I just didn't know how to help her. She was too afraid of Mark to say anything and was afraid that if she went against him, he would take Daisy and Jack and leave. Mark had been in contact with Sandy too and that is when he found out that she had lost her youngest son. Jason was born with an inoperable whole in his heart, heart disease and one valve to his heart was missing. He had to go in every few years and have a shunt installed to keep his blood pumping through his heart. Right before his ninth birthday, they had to go in and put in a larger shunt. They said that everything went fine but Jason never made it out of the operation room. Loosing Jason almost destroyed Sandy. She was not herself for a very long time but after Mark found out she had lost Jason, he offered to sell Jack to her for Five thousand dollars. Sandy called me and we talked about it. Knowing Mark had already sold two of his children we figured if Sandy didn't buy him, Mark would just sell him to someone else. Mark said he just wanted to help Sandy but we both knew it was really about the money. Sandy agreed to buy Jack and went through the adoption process to make it legal so he couldn't come and take him back. We got involved with a group of folks that square danced and it looked like fun plus it was a place that we could bring the girls along too. We made some pretty good friends there and we all did a lot of things together. Most of us had children close to the same age so it was easy to fall into friendships. After Sandy got Jack, she renamed him Jack and did her best to make him like Jason but Jack wasn't Jason and wasn't ever going to be Jason. I finally had a talk with Sandy and told her that she had always been so wonderful with children, but she was bordering on being abusive with Jack. She punished him constantly not realizing that she was expecting him to be like Jason. Fortunately, she listened to me and decided that she couldn't raise Jack. She just wasn't ready to raise a baby at the time because she hadn't healed or gotten over losing Jason. One of the couples that we square dance with were looking to adopt a child because but she couldn't have children. I approached them about adopting Jason and they were very excited about getting to adopt him. With them being some very good friends of ours, I was also able to keep an eye on him while he was growing up. I hadn't felt that it would be safe for me to keep Jason with me because I didn't trust Mark not to try and come and take him back.

Doug, my little brother showed up at our house one day and I looked to see who had brought him, but he said he hitched a ride out. Doug said that Karen (whom he lived with at the time) had packed up the whole house and left a couple cans of vegetables in the cabinet and nothing else. She left a note that said she was moving back in with her exhusband and Doug would have to figure out his own life. Doug was very angry with Karen and had decided that since she had been buying a car from my inlaws that he would come get that car because he felt like she owed him something. He was very angry with me too, thinking that I had known about what she had done but his telling me was the first I had heard. I tried to explain to him that the car did not belong to me and that my in laws would not release the car to him because he wasn't the one that bought it. He would not accept that answer and just kept getting madder and madder at me thinking that it was some scheme Karen and I had set up, but it wasn't. AJ and I offered to let Doug stay with us but told him he would have to get cleaned up and get a job. He said no, he wasn't willing to do that and left our house. I watched him walk away from my house down that dirt road and he never looked back. He vowed that Karen and I had done him dirty and that he would never speak to me again, that I was no longer his sister. He has kept his word and any letters or contact that I tried to make over the years has been refused. Some of the guys that lived out by us and some that we square danced with were on the Palmyra local volunteer fire department and were trying to enlist AJ to join. We both decided that it was something we were interested in, so we started attending the meetings and became volunteer fire fighters. I was the first female volunteer but most of the guys were cool about it. The assistant chief of the fire department did dirt work on the side to make extra money. AJ's job at the time was also doing dirt work (running heavy equipment) with Randy Kahle so they had a lot if common and him and his wife Anne became good friends of ours. AJ also worked on his off day with a good friend of our that was also a neighbor. They each bought equipment and worked the jobs they got in their off time from their other jobs. I became very good friends with Tami, his wife and we hung out a lot. We both liked playing cards and board games and we both had children close to the same ages, so it worked hanging out. Tami and I were friends for many years, and I counted on her friendship. We were closer that I was to my own sisters. Able to tell each other anything. After I had poured my heart out to TamI about how AJ was being gone a lot again and the girls and I hardly ever saw him. I started feeling more and more neglected and he never had time for the girls or me. The only time I ever existed to him was when he wanted to have sex. I felt like I was just a part of the furniture. After living this way for so many years, I just gave up on getting any loving attention from my husband. I tried to talk to AJ about my feelings and he said that he had been talking to one of the guys at work. Him and his girlfriend went to swinger clubs and thought that we thought should try that. It had helped their relationship stay exciting. We discussed it and decided that we would give it a try, Unfortunately, it didn't work out for us. AJ said that he couldn't relax enough knowing I was right there, and I was in the same position, I just couldn't relax enough to get anything out of it, so we decided that was a no go. After that, AJ decided that we needed to try an open marriage. That either one of us could date someone else. His reasoning was that we had gotten married so young that we never got to date other people and maybe that would help our relationship. I got asked out but wasn't interested in the guy that had asked so turned him down. AJ went out and he met a woman that he was interested in and wanted to go out with. During this time, people were making calls about products that they wanted to get your opinion on. I got one of those. They were asking about a laundry detergent and how often I used their product. They asked in I was married and if we had children. Later, I found out it was the woman that he had wanted to go out with, but he wasn't honest with her and didn't tell her he was married. She didn't want anything to do with him after that. In the meantime, I got a job that was during the night, AJ worked during the day, so we didn't have to worry about childcare. When Tessa was old enough to start school, working at night didn't work because I couldn't get home soon enough to get her ready and AJ had to leave too early. I tried to get a day shift job but there weren't any available, so I had to quit. I stayed home with the girls again and started looking for a job that would pay enough and I could work the day shift. AJ and I just were not getting along. He was rarely home and when he was, he was mean and said hateful, hurtful things to me. He still didn't have anything to do with the girls and I just couldn't take it anymore. I had a job in Baldwin and decided that I was going to move out and get a place of my own. I found a twobedroom trailer and the girls, and I moved there leaving AJ the house. I was working nights so was having to leave the girls alone while I was at work. I found out the girls were running wild from one of the local policemen that I was friends with, while I was working so I had to make them go back to the house with AJ when I was working. I was proud of myself for finally standing on my own but hated that the girls had to stay out at the house during the week, but I couldn't let them just run amuck. I think my leaving shocked AJ. He didn't think I would ever leave. He wasn't handling the separation very well and was talking to the girls about it and how much he loved me. AJ also apologized to the girls for the way he had been treating them. He cried when he talked about us being separated and that he just wanted us to get back together. God help me but I actually liked the fact that he wasn't being able to make it on his own. I was doing just fine, paying my rent and utilities and any other bills that I had. I took pride that in the first time I was on my own and responsible for myself that I was doing it and wasn't having to ask for help from anyone.

The girls felt so sorry for him and were always wanting me to give him another chance. They would tell me how he cried and told them that he loved them and me and that he just wanted his family back. I knew I was doing good and had even started dating someone. I could see the girls were struggling and I felt responsible for them so I stopped seeing the guy I had started dating and told AJ that I would move back in but that things had to change. He had already started trying to have a relationship with the girls, so I moved back and tried to make it work. AJ was different and attentive at first, but it didn't take long before he was right back to doing the same things he was doing before. Saying mean and hateful things to me, making me cry and telling me how fat and unattractive I was. I tried diet after diet but I just couldn't seem to lose the weight and I just wasn't able to make him happy. One of our friends told me to apply at the company they worked at. It would be days and they had very few women. They did underground installation on waterline, sewer line, and repairs. I developed crush on someone I was working with, but I didn't let him know. He was married and I didn't want to get in the middle of that, besides that, we were all friends. I finished off the summer, and then went to college during the school year. I figured, if I could work enough during the summer, I could save enough to go to college. I made it through my first year of college and when summer arrived, I went back to the construction company, but they wanted me to be a forewoman. I had had enough trouble with the guys on the crew that I knew they would not appreciate working for me or following my directions, so I turned down the position. They told me that I either came back as a forewoman, or they didn't have an opening for me. I was back to hunting for a job. AJ started working with a friend of his afterhours of his fulltime job and on the weekends, he was hardly ever home. I became friends with his partners wife, and we started hanging out a lot. I really liked her, she was tiny, cute and had a great sense of humor. She didn't much care for her husband either and we had a lot of conversations about our marriages. She told me that she saw other men and in fact sometimes more than one. I have to admit, I didn't care much for her husband either. AJ and him, were so much alike and had no time for family. One day while taking the girls to the swimming pool, I ran into Bob, the man I had the crush from the old construction crew, and we started talking. We ran into each other every once in a while and would visit while the girls swam. The company I was working for was moving to another town so my commute was going to be a lot further but I had made supervisor of second shift so got a nice little raise and that helped offset the cost of the gas to get there. Our family life and jobs were going fairly good. AJ wasn't around much and the girls had started middle school and were being bussed into the next town for school. We decided that the cost of where we were living was just too high and it didn't work for the girls either. They would be able to be more involved with school activities and I wouldn't have to constantly run them into town. Tessa was in band and Mary was in basketball. We started hunting for a house. We found one that we both liked that was in our price range. It needed some remodeling but was a large house with plenty of bedrooms. We had talked a lot about becoming foster parents and that house would be perfect with all the bedrooms it had. We sold our place and moved into town. We went to the Foster care classes and met some great people that we are friends with still today. They were actually going through the classes with the hope of getting to adopt eventually because they couldn't have children, but we just wanted to help not adopt. Once we made it through the classes, they called with a couple children and then a couple more and it seemed like they were always calling needing us to take more. I finally just had to learn to say no. We never had less than four children plus our two girls and that was plenty to take care of. I had also gone back to college and was working full time. The last two little ones we got, we had for a year and a half and got very attached to them. They went up for adoption after the year and a half and we talked about adopting them but realized that they needed way more help than we would be able to afford to give them so turned down the adoption. They both were adopted by a couple that couldn't have children and they were kept together so we felt it was meant to be. After that, we decided as the girls were getting older, we would only foster teenage girls. We didn't want any boys since our girls were getting older. Boys would only add to the problems. I had to make sure the foster children had their meetings with their councilors and get each child to their school activities. At this point we had made the decision to only foster older girls. I also felt that I had a lot to offer to young ladies that had been sexually assaulted and could help the understand that it wasn't their fault. One of the social workers asked me one day how do you do it? I replied that I really didn't know, that there were things that I knew had to be done so I just did them. The pain of having to hand a baby back over to the parents that had abused it was just doing a number on all of us including the girls. We fostered teenage girls for six years until one of the girls accused AJ of molesting her. All the girls were immediately removed from our home. They did an investigation, and I was able to prove that AJ wasn't even home at that time. She finally admitted that she had lied because she was mad at us but that ended us doing foster care because AJ just couldn't take the chance that it would happen again. During all this craziness, Tessa, our oldest daughter started dating one of the boys from her high school. They seemed to be getting serious about each other and I had always been very honest with the girls about sex. Even though I had talked to Tessa about waiting until she was older, I didn't trust that she would, so I made sure to provide her with birth control pills. I wasn't giving her permission to have sexual relations, but I knew I couldn't watch her twentyfour seven so added a little protection. Unfortunately, she was having relations with her boyfriend but wasn't taking the birth control pills and ended up getting pregnant. She was only fifteen at the time, too young to get married and her boyfriend wasn't willing to marry her anyway. He was denying that the baby was even his. AJ and I met with his parents, but it didn't do any good. I had to leave school and concentrate on helping my daughter through this. The high school she was attending told her she couldn't go to school there while she was pregnant because it just didn't look good. That she was an embarrassment and a bad example to the school so she dropped out and stayed home. Our granddaughter was born July 16th 1991. Tessa asked me to name her but she wanted her named after someone in the family. I came up with the name Jayde (Jay being AJ's middle name) and Lynnett for the middle name after Tessa's middle name Lynn.

One day I was trying to get the laundry done (which was in the basement). I was carrying a basket full of clothes in front of me because the stairs were thin. I got to the bottom step and when I stepped down, I stepped on one of AJ's boots and my ankle twisted and made a loud "pop" sound and then I went down on my knee. I wasn't able to get up and I didn't want to cry and scare the children, so I scooted on my butt all the way up the stairs and hollered for one of the older children. I needed them to call AJ because I was pretty sure my ankle was broken. AJ refused to come home. He told me to just call his sister and have her take me to the doctor in town, One, the doctor was an older man and I didn't want to go see him. I knew it was broken and I needed a cast. I finally called his sister, and she was on her way to get me when

AJ showed up. He was pretty pissed off and still insisted that we see the doctor in town. I told him no, he needed to take me to the hospital in Lawrence. He helped me get into the back of the van, lay on the floor and put my foot up on the back seat but he was so angry that he was driving too fast, breaking too fast and I swear, he hit every bump he could. Once at the hospital, they took me for exrays and yes, my ankle was broken. I was almost healed from that when I found out I had to have a hysterectomy. I was off work this whole time which I knew wasn't good, but I didn't have a choice. When I was finally able to go back to work, they told me that they had given my position to another lady by the name of Kathy, and she was even using my sign on of Kat. I tried to work for her, but I just couldn't deal with working for her.

The washing machine and dryer were in the basement and I was carrying a basket of dirty clothes one morning and did not see AJ's boots laying on the floor at the bottom of the stairs. When I stepped down that last step, I caught the sole of the boot laying on it's side causing my ankle to twist and me to fall down. I heard a loud pop when my ankle twisted and I was pretty sure from the pain I was in that it had broken. I had also landed right on my knee and that was extremely painful too. I tried to get up but couldn't so using my hands and the foot that didn't hurt, I started backing up the stairs on my butt. I tried to call for Tessa as she was the oldest and I thought she might be able to help me up the rest of the stairs. Instead one of the youngest girls heard me calling and when she saw I was hurt she started crying and calling for the other kids to come. I did not cry even though I really wanted to because I didn't want to scare them anymore than they were. I had Tessa give me the phone and I called AJ to tell him what happened and he said that there was no way it was broken and just to have someone take me to see the small town doctor. I told him no, that doctor was very nice but he was so old, I didn't trust him and that I needed to go to the hospital. He said that he was at work and couldn't leave so if I could, get his sister to come and get me and take me to the doctor. I called Kay his sister and she said she would come get me. Then AJ decided he would leave work and come after all so I had to call Kay and tell her to never mind. AJ was not happy that he had to leave work and was angry with me. He was upset that I wouldn't go to the local doctor and was not gentle when helping me get into the van. He was slamming on the breaks and hitting bumps and it felt like he was trying to make it hurt more because I had caused him such an inconvenience. That I should have been looking where I was going, and this wouldn't have happened. Now it was going to cost us more money because I had to go to the hospital. When we got to see the doctor in the emergency room, he took one look at my ankle and said yep, that's broken. They sent me to exray and then put a plaster cast on clear up to my knee. It was very heavy and painful. They sent me home with instructions to see my family doctor the next day. The swelling on the ankle and foot went down over night while it was up so the plaster cast was not fitting correctly and was very painful. My family doctor cut it off and gave me a plastic cast that you could pump air into. You could also take it off to bathe. It was so much lighter and much more comfortable.

I was off work while healing from the broken ankle because the job I had required you to be on your feet and I was not able to preform my tasks. While I was off work, I had to have my pap smear done and found out that I was going to have to have a hysterectomy and that I would have to take off even more time from my job. Work was not happy that I had to miss that much time but it couldn't be helped. I had the surgery once I was able to walk on my foot again. They told me that they removed my uterus but were able to leave my ovaries. They looked healthy and I wouldn't have to take any hormonal supplements. Things were tense at home. I wasn't able to work but was causing a bunch of medical bills. I had to be careful and not lift anything or do anything that would cause damage to the incision. They did not warn me that my hormones would go dormant because of surgery or the mood changes that would come with that. AJ came home in a foul mood one day after work going off about what a pigsty the house was. He was yelling and throwing things about the house. I did my normal thing, trying to appease him and ended up hurting myself (the incision) in the process. He saw that I had hurt myself and then started yelling at me for being stupid. I just could take anymore and started crying uncontrollably, went in and locked myself into the bathroom. AJ was yelling at me to open the door and let him in, that he wasn't mad at me but that the kids should have been helping out. I refused to open the door, partly because I was hurting and partly because I just couldn't deal with him at that time. He got mad that I wouldn't unlock the door and kicked it in. Once he was in the bathroom, he apologized for getting so upset and for making me hurt myself. He just held me while I cried and then helped me go lay down.

When I finally got released to go back to work, I called and let them know that I was officially released and could come back. They had me bring my release paperwork in and then politely told me that I no longer had a job. Thanked me for the time I had put in with them and said good bye. Wow! I hadn't seen that one coming. I got another job in Lawrence at a hardware/lumber yard and heard from one of the ladies that worked in the billing department that a brand new Walmart distribution center was being built in Ottawa and they paid great, the schedules were set so you always knew what days and hours you would be working. She had already been through the interview process and had given her notice at the lumber yard. I got the information of where to go to apply from her and went and filled out my application. There were also rumors that the hardware store was going to be shut down even though they hadn't even been open a year. I thought with my job history I would stand a good chance of being hired right away but I didn't receive any calls for an interview. I started calling them because

I desperately needed the job and that was the best option out there at the time. The lady on the phone told me that they had my application on file and would keep it for six months. I didn't need to call. If they were interested and wanted to hire me, they would call me. I didn't hear anything for several days and decided at that time to call them every day until they gave me an interview just to get me to quit calling. I did finally get a call for an interview and made it through that one and got a second interview scheduled fo the following week. I went through the second interview and they said that they wanted to go ahead and do the third interview right away if it would work for me. I said sure and went right into the third and then to the facility they had hired to get a Urine drug screen done. They told me if the drug screen was clear that I had a job waiting for me and they would call to let me know my start date. I was so relieved to know that I was going to have a job and that my workdays and times would always be the same. It was also a relief to know that I would have a decent paycheck coming in again. Walmart called and offered me was second shift unloading and processing fedex and ups trailers. I took it and was very happy to have the job. The lumber yard I was working for had just made the announcement that they were going to be closing the doors and going out of business. I felt so blessed to have a job to go to.

When I first went to work for Walmart there was no freight in the warehouse. We all practiced on the equipment to get licensed to run it. You had to watch safety films, take and pass a written test before you were allowed on any of the equipment and then had to put in numerous hours on the equipment before being issued a license to operate it. Once we had our licenses for the various pieces of equipment, they sent us out to a different part of the warehouse where everyone was on cleaning detail. The I beams had lain in the dirt before being put up and they had dirt inside them so they distributed buckets of water and soap with cloths and told us to scrub them down. We cleaned every day until freight started showing up. Then we would all crowd around a single pallet and take turns processing the freight so we could get the hang of how to identify what the freight was, that it matched what color it was supposed to be and that the count it was supposed to be packaged in was correct. We were taught how to read the bill of ladings and the purchase orders so we would know if we were receiving the correct freight. I was there for just under two months when a slotting position on day shift came open. That was someone that didn't do anything but process the freight. It was a day shift position and I didn't think I would stand a chance but I knew I wouldn't if I didn't try so I signed up for it. I was called into the office a week later and told that I had been awarded the position. I took pride in my work and was so grateful for having a job that I didn't complain or cause waves. I worked as hard as I could and if there wasn't anything to process, I helped unload the trailers. I had started working at the Walmart DC on second shift so I when I got home, I could get a little sleep and then get up to get the girls off to school and then try to get a little more sleep before I had to start my day over again. A job on day shift came up and I applied for it because I figured, what did I have to lose, I would either get it or not, but I definitely wouldn't, if I didn't try. I ended up getting the position, but it only lasted about six months and they promoted me to a supervisor position and put me right back on the night shift. It was amazing watching what happened in the distributions center. Most of the managers moved to Kansas from other states to open this center and it was like watching a soap opera. All the guys going after the women and the constant drama. There were several coaches that starting dating some of the hourly associates and some of them ended up getting married. Some ended up pregnant and then getting married. If you were in that click, you were ok because you got the good jobs but if you weren't, most of the time you were ignored or always stuck with the nasty jobs. There were several times that special projects came up and I noticed that the same two people always seemed to be the ones picked to do them. I asked to talk to the coach and let him know that other people were interested in doing some of the projects too and that maybe he should ask others to volunteer too. He thanked me and I went back to work; but he started being fairer about the special projects after that and many of us got a chance to do some of them. About two months after starting my slotter position on day shift, I was approached by the operations manager about becoming a supervisor. I thought it would be a great opportunity so said yes. When I was promoted, I was taken off the floor and put in the receiving office where the dedicated drivers brought loaded trailers onto the yard and then brought the paperwork to us to be processed. I worked in there for a few months then got transferred back out to the receiving floor. My cosupervisor (Sam) on the floor was constantly flirting with me even though he knew I was married and had told him that I had no interest in a sexual relationship but that I liked him as a friend. He would talk to me about different things and most of the time I could just laugh off what he was saying and didn't take him seriously. He did have a foul temper though and it didn't take much for him to start cussing people out. I tried several times to tell him that he couldn't do that. Walmart has a policy that there is no foul language. He would just laugh it off and tell me that I just didn't understand guys. That is how they talk to each other. I went to management to let them know what was happening and was basically told the same thing except they added that I just took things too personal. This went on for quite some time. One night the Operations manager was off duty and it was only us two supervisors on our dock. Toward the end of the shift, I went into the office to start the production sheets and was letting Sam finish up the business on the dock when I heard yelling. The door to the office was flung open and a clip board flew toward the wall hit it and came back at my face. Sam was yelling at one of the associates for bringing the cardboard from another dock to our dock to crush. The yelling and cursing got really bad, and I tried to step in and get him to stop. We wrapped up and went home but it bothered me all weekend how he had belittled that associate so badly and so on Monday I called the General Manager and told him what had happened and that I just couldn't keep working like that. He asked if I had ever spoken to upper management to let them know what was going on. I said that I had went to my Coach and then to the Operations manager but had been told that I was just taking things too personal. He wanted to know why no one had ever spoken to him with him about this issue and I told him that the policy states that we have to go through the chain of command and that is what I had been doing. The next morning, Sam was met at the front door and taken in to talk to the General Manager. They asked him about what had happened, and he admitted to everything. Since he was honest with them, they let him keep his job but demoted him. I was then called in and told that Sam had admitted to what happened and that he would still be working on my shift, but I was not allowed to talk about what happened at all. Mean time since he was demoted, he could talk to anyone about what happened and of course it was only his side. I was black listed by most of the people in the warehouse. When I would walk into a break room, everyone would stop talking. No one would sit with me and most times I was shunned. None of the other managers wanted to work with me and actually told me, when they had to work with me, that I had better not pull on them what, I had done to Sam. I told them that they didn't know what they were talking about because they only had his side of the story, but no one would listen. When I tried to tell the General Manager what was happening, he did not want to hear anything I had to say. I was miserable but I had lived through the abuse of my childhood, had always lived with rejection and not being accepted for just being me and I refused to let my place of employment break me. I kept my head up, still took pride in my job even when the other managers would disappear and leave the whole dock for me to run. No one would answer their radios, leaving me to assign and call out the trailers as well as handle any problems that came up I did it. I would not let them see me cry nor would I let them break me. I stayed in that position, doing my job until most everyone involved had either quit or moved away to another center. Then when an opening came up for a clerk out at the cross dock, I stepped down from my supervisor position and applied for that position. It was a separate building from the warehouse but on the same grounds. I felt like I had had so much pressure with all the responsibilities and now I was just able to go in and do my job and leave. The position was a step down from being supervisor, but all the pressure of the job was gone. The new position gave me the opportunity to go back to school and they let me work four ten hour shifts so I could have one day off to get all my homework done.

One day, I ran into Bob again and we were flirting with each other. We ended up having sex that day and I found out afterwards that it was his birthday. It wasn't anything that I had planned, it just sort of happened but I can't say that I was sorry it did. At least for a little bit, I felt attractive and wanted. TamI was married as well and was seeing several different men. When I told TamI about who I was seeing, she said that she was interested in him too. I told her, no way! I have had a crush on this man for a while now and she couldn't have him. TamI could and did have just about any guy she wanted. She had several relationships going at the same time even though she was married. I don't know how she kept them straight but would on occasion, stop at my house to clean up from being with one of them to go meet another. My relationship with Bob lasted about two and a half wonderful years. I felt loved and that I mattered to someone that didn't put me down or say nasty things to hurt me. After a couple years I started noticing little things like I saw TamI playing footsie with Bob in the hot tub. They moved pretty quick, so I wasn't sure, but it made me have doubts.

I had always told TamI everything. My problems with AJ and how I didn't feel like he loved me. TamI and I hung out all the time and we would set up date times for both of us to see our "other" men. I noticed that she flirted with all the guys and it didn't seem to bother her husband one little bit. Little things started catching my attention, like if we went on a hay rack ride, she would ride up on the tractor with Bob when he was driving, leaving Tammy, Bob's wife, her husband and her other man on the trailer. TamI would make comments about how I couldn't fit into her clothes and other unkind comments but she would make it into a joke, so it didn't seem like she was being mean. I saw Bob and her making eyes at each other and then one day after we all went on a hayride together, I heard her saying that she had lost her sitter and needed somewhere for her children to get off the bus until she could get home and wanted to know if it was okay if they got off with Tammy and Bob's kids until she could pick them up. That was a great big red flag for me. I knew right then what she was doing. She was scheming to be able to see Bob everyday. Tammy didn't get home until an hour or two after Bob so TamI would have all that time with Bob. I was sick to my stomach but knew I couldn't do or say anything. When our second Christmas came around, I got him what I could, but he had warned me to be very careful because his wife Tammy would notice. It was very difficult to get things she wouldn't notice so I tried to get things he could use in his office. We would make reservations at a motel in Kansas City to spend the day with the guys. The first year, we spent several hours before we had to go back. The next year, Bob made the comment that I got him almost the same thing as last year and didn't seem very happy with his gifts. I tried to explain that he told me I had to be careful and that made it very hard to know what to get him but one of the gifts I gave him, was that I had paid for the room so he wouldn't have to.

Bob seemed very anxious and not interested in having sex. When we did, it was very quick, and he was up and dressed and said that we needed to get back. He couldn't hardly stand the thought of TamI being in the motel room with Joe. Bob started calling their room and telling Joe that they had to go, that he had to get back to work. Joe was confused but they got ready, and we headed back to Baldwin. AJ and I went over to Tammy and Bobs house on a weekend to play cards and every time I even touched Bob, he would jerk away from me, like he didn't want me to touch him at all. Bob had told me many times that he loved me but that he wouldn't get a divorce because he lost everything in the first one and wasn't going to go through that again. He treated me so sweet when I was with him that I couldn't help but love him. I was so hurt and angry with what I was seeing between TamI and Bob that I thought about getting even with them. I told Joe my suspicions and told him that we should get together as a payback, but I was not able to. Joe is like a brother to me and sex with him just wasn't going to fix what was wrong. He didn't believe me anyway. He was so in love with TamI that he was ready to leave his wife and marry her. I decided to do the mature thing. and I bought a bouquet of beautiful yellow roses and went to Tami's work. I told her that I saw what I thought was going on and that if her and Bob had feelings for each other, that I loved them both enough to step back and let them be together. It hurt extremely bad but I thought that if they cared about one another I had no chance and didn't want to lose either of them. TamI swore up and down that there wasn't anything going on and that I didn't need to worry about that. Shortly after that we went to a party Bob and Tammy had at their house. It was already crowded by the time we got there, and I saw Bob and TamI sitting beside each other on the edge of a cow trough that they had set up as a pool for the kids to play in. They were as close as a tick on a hound dog. There were several people sitting around it so there wasn't any room for me to sit with them, so I hung out in the water with the kids. Bob got up and went somewhere so I sat beside TamI and tried to have a conversation with her, but she wouldn't hardly say anything. Then Bob came back over and in an angry voice, said "that's my seat, move". I just said okay and moved. They were sitting so close that there wasn't hardly any space between them. I knew then that he had made his choice and it wasn't me. Why does it seem everyone I care about always hurts me? Why does it seem that I am not worthy of being loved? I just couldn't understand what I had done that made me so unlovable? Why am I so broken? Bob never called and I didn't call him either. I figured he had made his choice and I didn't need someone in my life that could cheat on me with my best friend.

I know I had no right to be thinking about someone else the way I was, but I had lived my whole childhood wanting someone to love me and to make me feel that love. I was not very happy in my marriage because of the way AJ treated me. I was not good enough for anything but to have sex with. I couldn't seem to do anything to please him. The house wasn't clean enough, the dishes weren't always done, and if they were, it wasn't good enough. It was never good enough. I felt like I was reliving my childhood.

Back to the mental abuse but there was never any physical abuse. AJ never hit me, he didn't have to because his words cut me deep enough. He did think it comical when he would wake up before me and my thumb was in my mouth, he would shove it down my throat making me gag. He got a big laugh out of that. I never sucked my thumb when awake but there were times, I would wake up with it in my mouth. I was very unhappy but couldn't afford to move out again, so I moved upstairs, and AJ lived downstairs. Yes, I was still married to AJ and I know I had no right to be thinking about someone else the way I was, but I had lived my whole childhood wanting someone to love me and to make me feel that love. I had tried everything I could think of to make AJ love me, but I couldn't seem to make him happy. I was not good enough for anything but to have sex with. I couldn't seem to do anything to please him. The house wasn't clean enough, the dishes weren't always done, and if they were, it wasn't good enough. It was never good enough. I felt like I was reliving my childhood. Back to the mental abuse but there was never any physical abuse. A friend of ours suggested we see a marriage counselor he knew. He said she was really good, and you just paid her what you could afford. She met with you at her house because she was retired but still liked helping people that needed it. When we showed up for the appointment, I was amazed. She looked at AJ and asked him if he really loved me. AJ said yes that he did and that he wanted to work things out. She told him that if he really meant it then he had to do a lot of changing. That I had lived my whole childhood being abused and I just wasn't going to continue to allow him to do so too. There would not be another chance. 16 from bottom up: add a paragraph right after showing up for the appointment: new paragraph to add: She asked us what some of our issues were and she would try get a clear idea of what she could address what was tearing us apart. I told her about my abuse as a child and I felt that was what AJ was doing as well. I told her that he insisted on me getting my tubes tied. He's the one that told the doctor that I wanted to get them tied. I turned 19 years old a month after giving birth. Too young to understand how that was going to affect my mental health. I also told her about him shoving my thumb down my throat and how he got so much fun watching me wake up to having my thumb shoved down my throat. The constant verbal abuse and that he wouldn't ever help. It was all left up to me. How I always made sure there were gifts for everyone to open every single holiday and there was never anything for me. It didn't matter what holiday, I never got anything. She knew that I was done if it didn't work this time. I would not try to make it work again because I had discovered that I could take care of myself and didn't need to rely on someone to take care of me. She said that I had been through enough abuse, that some of the things he thought was funny like shoving my thumb down my throat was abusive and he was being a bully and that he better get it together because there wouldn't be a third time for me. This was it. He either change or he would be by himself.

She said so many things to him that I had not even realized I felt until they were spoken out load. She had him take a real good look at me and all that I had been through before him and asked him if he could take care of me like he should have been especially knowing all the abuse I had lived through. He said he could, and he would change and do whatever he had to do to keep our marriage together. She suggested that we start out by going on dates and get to know each other all over again and to pay attention to the things we did like about each other, build our relationship from there. AJ really did make some changes and I could see how hard he was working to make our relationship work. I sold my trailer and moved back into the house. We felt that if we were really going to work on our relationship that we both had to give it our all.

The hurt over the years was so painful. I was able to talk to my sisters about it and they both told me to leave him, but I was afraid to be on my own. I tried to lose the weight, but it just didn't seem to want to come off. During this time there were several guys at work that noticed me and a couple at the fire department too. They treated me like I was attractive and that I mattered. Most of the group we had been square dancing and would get together with drifted apart and the couple we placed Jack with would not have anything to do with us all of a sudden. They made excuses when we would try to set up a get together and once, after they made excuses on why they couldn't get together, we saw them out with another couple a few hours later. AJ confronted them and accused them of lying. If they didn't want to get together with us. then just tell us the truth. They didn't need to lie. They got very angry and cut off all contact. They wouldn't even let me see Jack after that.

When I did contact them about it, they said that when we went out on the boat that last summer, Sandy had shown up and they were upset that we went behind their backs and let her see him. We had not set that up and hadn't known Sandy was going to show up but when she did, we didn't see any harm. They said that wasn't for us to decide and they weren't going to let us see Jack anymore either.

I was so torn up over Bob and Tami, that I felt completely broken. All I could seem to do is cry. AJ kept asking me what was wrong, but I couldn't tell him. Why does it seem that I am not worthy of being loved? It seems like I give my all but I just get pain in return. I put all my concentration on work and learning everything I could. I volunteered for any training and any overtime that was offered. I insisted on learning how to do other jobs that I hadn't been trained in and was finally given permission to learn them. Once I did, they were constantly asking me to cover different positions and I worked a lot of double shifts. It helped keep my mind off the hurt, both from Bob and TamI and AJ. I just wanted to be loved for who I am but it just wasn't something I was ever going to find. I don't believe that there is such a thing as true love anymore. I have been hurt over and over and it didn't matter what I did to make them happy, they took and took but I didn't get anything in return but a broken heart. My size had nothing to do with who I am, and I wasn't that big. Size 18 is not obese, and my body build is not meant to be petit, and I never would be no matter how much I dieted. During this time, I decided to go back to college and get my diploma. I had a very busy schedule, working full time and raising my two daughters as well as helping Tessa with her baby. I have to give AJ credit. He was very much a hands on grandpa. Completely different than he was with his own children. He had no problem, feeding, changing diapers holding and playing with them.

At first AJ was very supportive of my furthering my education. We got the money together to pay for my class each semester, so we didn't have to take out any loans. Further into taking my classes, I got the opportunity to take more than one class at a time. A friend of ours started taking classes at the same college and we decided if we carpooled, we could save a little money.

It seemed that the further I went with my classes the more AJ started putting more and more obstacles in my path. He would say hateful things about how I didn't do enough around the house, that I was gone all the time and if I was home, all I did was homework. He said we couldn't afford to pay for the classes anymore and was trying to force me to give it up. I decided that getting that diploma was very important to me and I wasn't going to let him make me quit. It was the first thing that I was doing just for me. It was extremely difficult to study at home and the tensions between AJ and I was so distracting that I started staying at school more and more. It was quiet there and easier to study and a couple of the classes I was taking were very difficult so a few of us would get together and do group study. Tessa and Jayde moved out to a small house just down the block at this time. She thought that she wanted to start standing on her own but didn't go so far that she couldn't ask for help when needed. Mary was a junior in high school. We had stopped doing the foster care so there weren't any children left at home that needed my care. It was my time to do something for me and I just wasn't going to let anyone stop me. I went and talked to the school counselor, and they helped me apply for scholarships and student loans. I was awarded a scholarship and what that didn't cover, the school loans did. AJ was very mad at me for borrowing the money, but I was too close to graduation to stop now. The homework kept my mind occupied, and we had decided to sell the house in Baldwin and move closer to Ottawa. The Baldwin house was just way too big for us now. It was made for a lot of children and we had none. I was working and taking my classes, just trying to keep going. I graduated in 2001 with an Associates of applied science degree in business. In 2002/2003

AJ and I decided that we were going to hire a private investigator to find my baby brother that was born after we were sold. I wasn't sure if there was really any chance, but I felt that I had to at least try. I gave the investigator all the information that I had, and he said he would help me for $150.00 dollars but that I would have to do part of the work. That sounded good to me, so he told me where to start searching on the internet for information. I just kept coming to dead ends and got very frustrated. I called the investigator and informed him that I was very upset and nothing I tried was working. I wanted my money back and was going to just forget it. He told me to calm down and to let him see what he could come up with first. A couple of weeks later, he called and said he understood why I was so frustrated! He was coming up with dead ends too, but he was going to get his assistant in on it too and they would do the research themselves. Something was just not right about what they were finding. It took one and a half years for the information to be put together. The private investigator finally gave me a call and set up a time for my husband and I to meet him and go over the results. When we met with him, he had some documents and said it had been a very difficult trail to follow but had finally gotten what they found to be very interesting results. Apparently, my birth father went by two different last names at different times in his life. His death certificate was under the name of Sayers and Chapman in different States. The birth and death dates were identical. With further investigation, it looked like he randomly changed his name to one or the other when they moved from state to state.

He also found out that my birth mother was still alive and that I had two brothers not just one and they were all living in the same town in Fort Mohave Arizona! The investigator also showed me that right after they sold my siblings and myself, they got remarried under the name of Sayers.

I called my sisters and let them know what I had found out and told them I was going to write a letter to them. In my letter, I explained that I didn't want anything from them other than some information and the chance to meet them. I waited on pins and needles to hear back and then one day I got a call from my birth mother and she said that she wanted to see us and that she had told our younger two brothers all about us. Of course, what she had told them was that we were given up for adoption. She didn't tell them the true story of having sold us. Karen could not get away at the time, so Sandy and I booked a flight and rented a car and motel room to go meet the mother that I had no memory of, but that Sandy remembered with so much pain (because she had been seven or eight when she let her go) and the brothers that we had never met. Once there, we met with them that evening in the lobby of our motel and set up a breakfast date with just our mother to have some, one on one time with her. It was at that time (going off the paperwork from the investigator) that I asked her how much they got for all of us kids. She said "why I would never do such a thing! your dad had wanted to sell you, but she said no." I knew at that time she was lying. She said that "they couldn't afford to take care of us so advertised us in the newspaper and some people came and got us." Part of why I knew she was lying is because she kept referring to the people that they sold us to by their first names and had way too much knowledge of them to have been strangers.

My birth father had been a pedophile and had sold us to a pedophile and our mother had just let him do it. I asked Anita if we had any other family that we could contact. She said there wasn't anyone left that she had lost contact with them many years ago so couldn't tell us anything but where they were living the last time, she saw them. At that time Anita looked at Sandy and said you know, you were the hard one to give up (I felt like I hadn't mattered to her at all) and then she showed us a few pictures that she had kept of Sandy, Mark and Karen but there wasn't a single picture of me or Doug. We met with each of the brothers during the day and then we all had dinner together that night. Right before going to dinner, Joe (my youngest brother) pulled me aside and asked if him and Anita could come live with me. I was really surprised at that question and said no. I didn't know these people. I know were related but I had never met them before and what I did know about them, did not make me want to let them move in and live off of us. Neither one of them had a job, they were both heavy smokers and I didn't need more people to take care of. The boys paid for dinner that night and we all planned on meeting again the next morning before Sandy and I had to head back home. As we were all getting ready to go our separate ways, they asked to borrow money from us because they needed gas to get Anita to the emergency at the hospital to see a doctor because she was having an episode, problems breathing, and they were worried about her. Sandy and I gave them the money and then we all went to the hospital to make sure she was going to be ok. She was released after a couple hours and told to go home and relax. The strain of the last couple of days had just been too hard on her. Sandy and I had to head home but said we would keep in touch. Over time, the boys did send the money they borrowed back.

Mary only had to take a couple of classes for her senior year for a semester to graduate but the small town we lived in didn't offer that kind of a program. Mary had to decide if she wanted to finish out her senior year where her friends were or if she wanted to go live with her aunt and just do the one semester. As Mary had never been really social, there were only a couple of very close friends and she knew that if she only went for one semester, that would give her more time to work and save up some money. Mary had signed up to go into the marines after graduation but she wouldn't be eighteen until August so could work and save up some money before then. She chose to move in with her Aunt, finish school and work until it was time to go into the marines. It was so hard to see her growing up and making such important decisions for herself. Tessa met a young man at Walmart. They worked together on the same dock and had hit it off. She started dating him, brought Doug to meet the family and Jayde. Doug seemed a very nice, good looking man that had a good job and he treated Tessa and Jayde well. They were in a big hurry to get married and set the date for a few months out but kept moving it up. At first, we thought maybe she was pregnant again but no she wasn't. They said that they were just so much in love and just couldn't wait to start their lives together. They were married just a few months after meeting. With both of them working at Walmart, they were doing very well and moved to a larger apartment. After a few months, Doug got word that his dad was not doing well. That he was very ill and there wasn't anyone there to help him. Doug's mom and dad had divorced years ago. His mom and sister had moved to Topeka Kansas where his mother's twin lived. Doug filed for a transfer from the Walmart dc in Ottawa to the grocery DC in Kentucky so they could move out there to help his dad. Within the same week of the kids packing up and leaving, Mary left for boot camp in North Carolina. I spent a week crying my eyes out! Talk about empty nest syndrome!! All the kids gone at the same time and no way for me to contact either one. I couldn't just run over and give them a hug or a kiss. I couldn't even call because Tessa and Doug had to be careful of the minutes on their phone and with Mary in basic training, she was not allowed any communication with her family or friends.

Jack showed up at our house out of the blue one day to give us an invitation to his graduation party. He was graduating high school and his mom said he could invite anyone he wanted to, and he wanted us there. He said that after the party his mom told him he had to move out that night, that her obligation to him was over. Even though we didn't hang out with any of the couples that would be at the party any longer and did not feel welcome at his parents' home, we went because we wanted to show Jack that no matter what we were still there for him once he moved out of his parents' home. We kept in contact with each other and what was going on in each other's lives. Jack asked me about his birth parents and wondered if I still had any contact with them. He was interested in finding them, but I told him that I didn't want him anywhere near Mark. I was afraid that Mark would get him into trouble or would end up using him. Teresa his mother had not willingly given him up and I would do what I could to help him find her and his sister Daisy but didn't know for sure how because I didn't know if Teresa had changed her last name. The last I heard from Sandy was that Teresa had called her and told her that Mark had left her and when Teresa asked about Jack, Sandy panicked and didn't know what to say because she had never told them that she didn't keep him. Jack said that he wanted to think about it and if he ever decided to look for them, he would let me know.

AJ and I were out hunting for a piece of property out in the country that I had seen advertised, close to the Walmart distribution center. We went and looked at it but neither of us liked the looks of it. We drove around on the country roads for a while before we decided to head back home. We stayed on the back roads though just taking in the scenery when we saw a for sale sign. It looked like a nice piece of ground but didn't have a realtor name or phone number listed. The neighbors that lived next to it were home. I told AJ to drive up and ask them if they knew who owned it. He didn't want to at first, but I talked him into it. Thank goodness I did! The people next to the property said that it belonged to his mother. She had bought fifteen acres and had planned to build out there but had changed her mind so was selling it off in five acre lots. Two of the lots had already sold, one to them and the only one left was the corner lot. They gave us her number and said to give her a call, they would let her know to expect to hear from us. We called her that next day and made a deal on the property. The dirt work on getting the basement dug was started but the first snows hit before we got very far.

Mary finished basic training so we were going to her graduation. We stopped and picked up Tessa, Doug and Jayde on our way. It was so good to see them! Jayde was getting so big! We went on to North Carolina to see Mary and watch her graduate. It was so amazing to see her and what a grown woman she had become. I almost couldn't recognize her, not only had her appearance changed but she was respectful and polite where before she didn't care what she said or who she hurt saying it. It was like she was a completely different person, and I liked the changes! We got to watch all the marching, graduation and to visit with her for a couple days but then we had to go home, and she had to go do her marine stuff. It was so hard to let her go again but I could see the good it was doing her. She really liked being in the Marines. We took the kids back to Kentucky and dropped them off with more tears and headed back to the house. Tessa called just a couple of weeks later and said her and Jayde were coming home. Doug was staying behind to pack up everything and would follow. He just couldn't stand working at the grocery DC and had quit his job and they didn't have any money to live on. Of course, I told them to come home but I couldn't understand why Doug would just quit and not try to get a transfer back to the distribution center in Ottawa. Tessa couldn't explain it, other than to say he didn't get along with his manager and got mad one day and walked out. Tessa then told me she was pregnant again and she just wanted to come home to be around her family. We picked Tessa and Jayde up from the bus stop and brought them home. Doug followed a couple of weeks later with his dad's truck loaded, but for some reason, he had left half their stuff at the apartment they had been renting. He only had part of their clothes and pieces of the furniture wasn't there. When we asked him why he left all that stuff he just said that he was in a hurry to get back to his family and it was just stuff that could be replaced anyway.

We didn't like his answer or his reasoning but there was nothing we could do about it. Doug said his dad gave him the truck, but we found out later that wasn't the case. "Doug had just taken it and they were looking for it. It got repossessed and taken back to Kentucky."

The kids stayed with us for a time while Doug was looking for work. When he was able to get a job and they could get their own apartment and move out. I loved my daughter and granddaughter but didn't really care for Doug much. He seemed lazy and didn't pick up after himself. Tessa was always making excuses for him. He would go into the kitchen, fix a big meal for himself, fix his plate and go into the living room to eat it and watch TV and just leave the everything on the stove. He never put the food away, would leave his halfeaten plate of food on the coffee table and soda cans scattered everywhere on the furniture. I asked him over and over to not set his soda cans on my furniture, that it would leave rings, but he totally ignored my requests and kept doing it. We didn't charge them rent or ask for any help with the utilities or groceries because we wanted them to be able to get a place of their own, so the wastefulness was even more aggravating.

Doug was always making smart aleck remarks and thought he was funny. I did my best to keep the peace for the sakes of my daughter and granddaughter but was very grateful when he finally got a job, and they were able to move into their own place. After Tessa gave birth to another little girl she named Randi Kathleen Nicole, she got a job at a local small family restaurant. I would stop by every once in a while, and sometimes if it was really busy, I would help by bussing the tables or pouring more coffee so she could have a couple minutes to visit with me. Her boss was new to the family type restaurant but had experience in a pizza restaurant. He asked a lot of questions and Tessa quickly made manager and got a much needed raise with it. Her boss was also asking me a lot of questions about how to do different barbeques, and how to do some of the homemade dishes that I cook. He approached me with an offer of partnership to go into business with him. I wouldn't have to come up with any money but would take over the morning shift. Make homemade biscuits and gravy and my homemade cinnamon rolls as well as some casserole type dishes for the day. In exchange, I would draw a salary and be part owner. I talked to AJ about it, and we decided it that we would do it. AJ came to the restaurant several times to help with the barbeque part and we brought in our power washer and really gave the kitchen a good cleaning. It was a very busy time because we were both still working full time. AJ and I had joined a camping group and would have a scheduled camp weekend once a month during the summer. We had several friends in the group and it was a welcome break from the craziness of normal life. We would either cook out or go to restaurants as a group, play board and card games and just enjoy life. Sometimes we would all go canoeing. We looked forward to those weekends because it was so relaxing and fun to visit. We rarely missed a camp out and every year they had a vote to see who would become the secretary, and who would be the one to set up all the camp reservations. Everyone voted that I become the secretary because the one that had been doing it couldn't anymore. I didn't really want to do it, but everyone kept saying I needed to. One of the couples that we thought were good friends with us was upset because they thought that they should have been voted in as secretary. Plus, they were very attached to Ryanne and thought that they should be able to have her whenever they pleased. I would not have had a problem with that, but we had found out Ryanne was allergic to ciggerette smoke and they were extremely heavy smokers. I told them they could have her but they would need to smoke outside. They agreed to that and then when the group went out for dinner, they asked if Ryanne could ride with them. I said yes as long as they didn't smoke with her in the vehicle. We passed them on the highway and all three adults in the truck were smoking! When we got to the restaurant, we had Ryanne come sit They started excluding us on the plans for the day and would just disappear. We were no longer invited over to play games and then other members of the camp group started avoiding us as well because they didn't want to make anyone mad at them. I was hurt because I hadn't wanted the secretary position to begin with but if that was all it took to start treating me bad and exclude me from what was going on, they weren't much in the way of friends to begin with.

Mary had gotten assigned to Twentynine Palms in California and seemed to be doing very well. She didn't like it as much as she had liked basic training, but she was dealing with it. She had made some friends, was doing some traveling and sightseeing on her off days. She sent some pictures of the scenery and told us that she loved and missed us. We kept her up to date on all that was going on at home. One day Mary called and said that she needed to let us know she was pregnant. She was twentyone by now and she was not going to marry the father. He drank too much and when she told him that she was pregnant and that he had to stop drinking, he told her no. Mary decided to have her baby and raise it on her own. The Marines would not represent her on child support because the father was a Marine also and they were representing him. Mary's commanding officers kept telling her that she either needed to marry the father or have an abortion because she was an embarrassment to the Marines. She refused and after several attempts on the Marines side, they left her alone until after the baby was born in October. Then they tried to make her give the baby up for adoption. When she refused to do that, she was given a transfer to Okinawa Japan and told she would not be able to take her baby with her. Mary filed several do not comply forms but was told that if she didn't go then she would go to the brig and the baby would go into state custody. I told her to just shut her mouth, bring me her baby whom she had named Ryanne and get her time served so she could get back here to her. Mary brought me her little girl at five months old and shipped out. I was still working the evening shift at Walmart distribution center. I took care of Ryanne in the mornings and then had to take Ryanne to childcare for the afternoon. When AJ got off work, he would pick Ryanne up and take her home feed, bath and play with her until he put her to bed. AJ was so different with Ryanne and our other granddaughters than he was with our own daughters. He was really good with them and played with them. During the time we had Ryanne, we decided to sell the house in Baldwin. We started the dirt work on the land we bought in Ottawa before winter hit and it was time to start building on the five acres again not that the weather had cleared up. The new house was much closer to Walmart so I wouldn't have so far to drive to work and school. We parked the fifthwheel out on the property while we were building. We built our house by putting up a large building and framing the house inside of the building. Then we planted many fruit and shade trees, had a large garden that we were able to put vegetables up. With Mary not taking any time off, she was able to complete her service and get back to Ryanne right before Ryanne's second birthday. Mary moved back in with us to give Ryanne time to get to know her and to develop a mother daughter relationship. We completely stayed away from the group of people we had previously hung out with. It was too painful for me to be around them. We would hear through the grapevine that they were going on family vacations together and spent a lot of time together. I just kept trying to concentrate on work and learning everything I could. Many days I would work double shifts to keep myself busy and my mind off the hurt that they had caused me.

Once Mary moved back in it was obvious that she wanted to have a relationship with Ryanne but she had so much guilt for having left her when she was so little. It was not Mary's choice to leave her baby and she shouldn't have felt guilty, but she did, and she was constantly buying Ryanne stuff to try and make up for it. I tried to tell her that isn't what Ryanne needed. It didn't seem like their relationship was developing into a mother daughter relationship the way it should have been. It was more like I was the mother to both of them and they were sisters. Mary approached AJ and I and said that she had been thinking about it for quite some time and thought that she would like for AJ and I to go ahead and adopt Ryanne. She talked to other close family members about it too and they were all having a fit and saying bad things about her being able to give up her child even if it was to her own parents, so she decided not to let us adopt her. Mary lived with us for about three years and worked at Kmart warehouse. In hindsight, we realize now that it would have been better if she had taken Ryanne and moved into her own home. I think their relationship would have been much stronger and Ryanne would have adjusted to Mary being her mother. Mary worked the night shift and spent so much time running back and forth from our house to child care and then to work she accepted an offer from the child care to rent a room from them. They moved out and stayed there for about six months and then decided that wasn't such a good idea and moved back home with us while she was planning to go to school to become a Registered Nurse.

Tessa lost her job at the family restaurant and Doug didn't have a job either so they ended up moving to Topeka and living with his mother and stepfather while trying to get on their feet again. Tessa got a job at a fastfood restaurant and Doug would get odd jobs. Tessa would call every once in a while and tell me she needed help financially. They didn't have any food or were going to be kicked out of their apartment and didn't have anywhere to go. We had already helped them so much that they were into us for 15,000.00 dollars. AJ ended up using all his inheritance from his parents to pay off a car that we had cosigned for them when they both had good jobs and they promised to pay off. We finally had to say no more, or they were going to take us down with them. I would take over food every now and then though because I didn't want my grandbabies to go hungry. I worried because Jayde didn't look right. I kept trying to tell Tessa something was wrong. Tessa would just tell me that it was just growing pains and she was fine, but I knew better. I just didn't know what it was. Tessa finally took Jayde to the doctor to," as she says shut me the fuck up" and they ended up rushing her to Children's' medical hospital in Kansas City. Her blood sugar was off the charts. The nurses could not believe she wasn't in a coma. Jayde had just turned nine years old and was diagnosed with type 1 diabetes and was insulin dependent. They kept her in the hospital for a few days and made sure she knew how to give herself her shots.

I was still working out at the CenterPoint office for Walmart and taking several computer courses when one of the reports that we had to fill out on every load that came in the office with all the purchase order numbers being handwritten so I decided to set up a computer program to record the information. Once I had it completed and was able to show how much better it was then the handwritten report and how it could be shared with all the clerks it was presented to management and rolled out as the new report that they would all use from then on. In fact, I found out later that they had rolled it out Walmart wide and they were all using my program. Of course, I didn't get anything for creating it. I don't know who got the credit for the program but it wasn't me. They had an opening in the dispatch office I applied for as a driver coordinator. I loved the position and got very good at it. Any time there was any training, I was sent to Bentonville to get the training and would come back and train everyone else. I was told with my degree and experience I should apply for a position at the Regional Operations Center in Bentonville, Arkansas. It would be a great promotion even though it would mean having to move. I made it through most of the interviews with no problem and got passed on to the third and final interview. I just knew I was going to get that job but when the third person came on the phone line and told me who they were I knew any hope of getting the position was gone.

She was the wife of the Operations manager that had gotten in trouble for not handling the problem with Sam when I was out on the dock. She even asked me if I remembered her husband before she told me that she didn't feel that I qualified for the position. An opening came up in the dispatch office not long after that and I applied for it. I was offered the job and moved into dispatch to work. I loved that job! I got to work with the Walmart drivers, update their trip sheets and make sure their pay was correct. Everything I was doing in that office just clicked for me and I got very good at what I was doing. I worked the third shift by myself and took pride in being able to perform all tasks. Even those that were not in my job description. I never had to call a manager for any issues that came up during the night but would figure out how to fix it on my own. Tessa called one day and said that Jayde was in the hospital again. It seemed like every few months she was in the hospital. I knew she wasn't getting fed the way she should have been and Tessa wasn't giving her the insulin shots like she was supposed to because they couldn't afford them. I had taken food to them to make sure the kids weren't going hungry but the next day when I went back over, the house was full of people and Tessa had cooked the food I took over and was feeding a bunch of their friends. When I asked her what she was doing and that I had brought that over for the children, she said that she was repaying these people for helping them out when they needed it. I was so frustrated and knew that even taking over food was not going to help. Doug was hooked on meth and I know Tessa was doing some as well as smoking pot. That is where their money was going. Tessa at least worked a lot but Doug wouldn't hardly work. He was too good to flip hamburgers, so he hung out at home or with his buddies and got high. This last time Jayde went into the hospital, I turned Tessa and Doug in for medical neglect. I was so scared that my granddaughter was going to die from not getting her insulin and not being fed correctly. Her kidneys were failing. Child services wanted to know if I was seeking custody of the children and I told them no, that I just wanted to make sure that Tessa and Doug understood how serious this was and that they could lose the children if they didn't get their acts together. I didn't want to take their children from them but to grow up and raise their own children and take Jayde's disease seriously. Tessa got very angry with me for turning them in and refused to speak with me or to let me talk to or see our grandchildren for two and a half years. The only reason she gave in to letting us see them at that time was because the girls insisted that they wanted to see us and Tessa finally gave in.

One of the nights I was working, I had a driver from another city come in for a load going out of the distribution center but he said he wasn't going to be able to gate until the morning. I explained that if he couldn't gate with the load that I would have to take the load off of him because there would be drivers coming in that would have the hours to get off the yard with the load. He got very angry and said that no, I wouldn't be taking the load off him and to give him the bills and he would go out on the yard, take his layover and depart in the morning. I refused to give him his bills and another driver had come into the office and overheard the conversation. He told the original driver that I was telling him the truth, that I couldn't leave the load on him if he wasn't going to gate. The driver then started cussing at me and yelling and tried to brow beat me into giving him the bills. I wouldn't do it and he stomped out of the office. The next day when I came in to work my shift, I was called into the General Managers office and asked about what had happened during the night and if I had had words with a driver. I said that I had and what I had done to handle the situation and he said he just wanted to let me know that asset protection had overheard the entire conversation. It was reported that I had stayed professional during the whole confrontation. He also informed me that the driver had been released from Walmart. I was shocked! I wouldn't have ever said anything about what had happened and now a longtime driver was out of a job. When I went back out to my desk to start my job, the day shift girls were giving me the stink eye and treating me as if I had some kind of disease. Then different drivers started approaching me throughout the day and asking what I had done and that they heard that I had gotten a driver fired. I did my best to explain that I had not done anything. The driver did it to himself by yelling and cussing because he didn't get the load that he wanted and that I had not turned him in. Someone else that overheard him had so he had done this to himself.

Drivers stopped asking after a few weeks and the other coordinators finally started treating me better. After five years my Operations manager came to talk to me and said that I had been doing a managers' job for the last five years and they felt that I need to promote up. All my previous evaluations had all been exceeds expectations and that just wasn't heard of. In order to promote, I would have to move to Bentonville, Arkansas. I went home and told AJ what they had said and what kind of a pay raise that would mean.

We decided that it would be a good move for me but with Mary going to school and living with us, he wouldn't be able to leave until she graduated. That meant that I would be living in Arkansas for the next five years by myself. We had promised her we would help her, and we wanted to make sure she would be okay. I felt that it would be good for me to get away from the situation with Bob and Tami, even though I never saw them. I was hearing through the grapevine that they were all going on family vacations together. Going skiing and hanging out together all the time. It was just adding more pain upon pain. I threw myself into work and kept myself busy with that. I was putting in so much time and learning new things to keep my mind off of my hurt so the promotion came at a good time for me.

Later on, I heard that while they were on one of their double family vacations that Bob and TamI had gotten caught and that ended that as far as I know. I didn't try to stay up with either of them, but it wouldn't surprise me if they kept seeing each other anyway. They were both very good at sneaking around to spend time together.

I accepted the promotion and moved to Arkansas to work in the Regional Operations Center. The exact same position that I had been told I was not qualified for five years previously. AJ and I went to Arkansas to find me an apartment, to stay in until he could move with me. We looked to see if there was a place, we could park the camper but all the camping sites were too far out from where I was going to be working so decided that an apartment would be better. We were able to find a decent apartment not too far from where I would be working, and I moved in. It was very lonely being there by myself. I didn't know anyone to hang out with and on the weekends, the people I worked with had family and friends of their own they wanted to spend their time with. I worked the night shift and so had to try and sleep during the day. I had to try to keep that schedule even on my off days or the 1st couple of nights of work were really tough. Most of the people in the apartment worked days and were home at night so that worked out well for me except on my off days. Getting any sleep was almost impossible with people running in and out and lawn mowers mowing. I decided that I just couldn't do the apartment thing and needed to find a house where I could at least get some sleep. I started house hunting and then when I found a couple that I thought would be good to look at, AJ would come down on the weekend and we would go look at houses. I found one in Bella Vista that I loved and one in Rogers that was okay. The negative on the Bella Vista house was that the front yard was the side of a mountain and would be impossible to get up or down if it was icy out and it was a long drive to get to Bentonville where I worked. The house in Bentonville was 4bedroom, 2.5 bath and so close to work. I could walk if I needed to but was going to need a complete remodel. Since AJ was not going to be there most of the time, we chose the house in Bentonville because it was so close to work. As a manager, I found out at the end of the year, I got a bonus. The first year, most of the money was spent on remodeling the house. AJ came down every weekend he had off to get the house stripped and remodeled. We donated as much of the supplies out of the house (cabinets, paneling, & sinks) to habitat for humanity to help fix up houses for those in need. It ended up being a very pretty home when we got done, that I didn't mind living in at all. AJ doesn't like living in town though and so I had to keep looking for some property that we could build on when he was able to move to Arkansas with me. It seemed that living and being so far apart, actually made our marriage stronger. AJ was so different when we did get to see each other. He did comment one time about my weight on one of the visits home but he dropped it after that. He made me feel more important to him and showed that he had really missed me. He was more attentive, and he was very loving. He would sit and hold my hand in the evening while watching TV. Once the house in Bentonville was done, we went back to me traveling to Kansas most of the time because I got three days off while he only got two. With me traveling there I also had the opportunity to see the kids', so it worked out better that way. In 2009 I finally found a flat enough piece of land just on the outskirts of Rogers Arkansas that we would be able to build on. It looked awful because it had become a dumping ground like a junk yard. It was extremely overgrown with weeds so the realtor and I were only able to walk so far onto the property. There was an old log cabin and an old garage that was more of a shack that was on the property but we couldn't get any further back to see if there was anything else. When we got back in the car, we looked at out laps while putting on our seatbelts and noticed we had ticks all over us! We both jumped back out of the car jumping around and brushing at our clothing and each others backs! We were both so grossed out, we kept looking to make sure we didn't miss any. AJ hadn't moved to Arkansas yet, but we felt that we needed to buy the property while it was there. The property was on foreclosure and we offered the bank what they were asking. We decided to build a building house for the time being and then later when the house in Bentonville sold, we would be able to build a real house in front of the building. AJ moved to Arkansas in 2010. AJ didn't worry about getting a job right away because he needed to clean off the property that we had bought. We had all the heavy equipment to clean it off ourselves and there were many times people would stop and just watch him work. We had two fire departments come out to get the log cabin burnt down. We had wanted to save it but it was in such bad shape there wasn't any way we could. The fire departments came out and started fires and then put them out most of the day. That night, they finally let the fire go and burnt it down. Unfortunately the housing market hit bottom and we weren't able to sell the house in Bentonville so ended up living in the building house which was nice enough. One of the people that was watching AJ work, ask him if he had a job and AJ said just what he was doing. They were impressed with watching him and ask him to come in and apply for a job. AJ had applied for jobs in several places. They always told him he was overqualified. He told them he didn't care what he was paid, he just needed a job but didn't have any luck. The job they had for him was working with a paving crew. The first year, they had him holding signs for the traffic flow. He hated doing that and his feet hurt so bad by the time he got home, he couldn't hardly walk. One day, on one of the jobs, there was some equipment that needed to be off loaded of a big flat trailer. No one was there to unload it, so AJ got up in the machine, looked over the controls and figured out how to operate it. He unloaded the trailer and the other guys kept saying that he had run a machine like that before, but he hadn't. Then on another day, the paver operator got mad and walked off the job. None of the other guys knew how to operate it so they asked AJ if he thought he could park it. He said I can try. He got on the machine, checked out the controls and figured out how to back it up. The boss was so surprised because he had backed it up perfectly. He asked AJ if he would be willing to try to run it the next day and AJ said he would give it a try. He did such a beautiful job.

They took pictures of the road and that is what they use for their advertisements. From then on, he was the operator until we had to move. After that, AJ figured out that I would get a bonus at the end of the year but I never really got to see much of it. I insisted that I got enough to get all the dogs shots and medications for the year but after that, it was all spent. There was always a credit card or something that had to be paid and the only way we could do it was use my bonus.

The local high school contacted us and ask if we would be willing to participate in a student exchange program and we thought it would be interesting so decided to do it. I worked nights so we decided we would take on one boy. We were sent a group of pictures of kids and picked out the one that we thought would work best for us because he had a similar background. We ended up with two boys though because they had one fifteen year old, boy that they couldn't find a place for. They offered to just have him stay with us for a few weeks and would move him once they found another home. I told them no, if I take him, it would be for the full school year. I couldn't see moving a kid around when he was already in a strange country and didn't know anyone. We had so much fun with them, but it was a lot of work too. The boys were complete opposites and didn't get along very well. We decided even though we had loved having the boys, we didn't want to do it again.

I lived in Arkansas for ten years and AJ was there for five when I got a promotion and had to move to Plainview Texas. Let me tell you, its aptly named! We really wanted to keep the property that we had built on but with the house in Bentonville not selling AJ decided to stay there and just have me move to Plainview by myself. We both knew I only had to put in two years and then would be able to transfer to another location when a position opened. I had to be there within a couple weeks, so AJ and I decided to find a RV park and take the motorhome down for me to live in. I didn't want to go all the way to Plainview by myself! I was trying to pack what I thought I would need into the motor home, crying the whole time. AJ came back from work a couple days later and announced that he quit his job and he would move with me. I was so excited! He cared about how upset I was and had done that for me! I thought he was moving with me because he loved me and didn't want me to be there by myself. When we pulled into the RV park, I was in shock! It looked like a junk yard! I wasn't very excited about being there without AJ. He had to go back to Rogers Arkansas and get all our stuff packed and moved. That was a big mistake because if he didn't think we needed it, he threw it away. I ended up missing so much of my kitchen stuff, it was unbelievable! AJ finally made it to Plainview, and he hated living at the RV part too, so we got serious about finding a house. There were a lot of houses for sale, but way out of our budget. We finally found a doublewide trailer, out in the country, but not too far from town and it was on eight acres. Already fenced off for cattle and there was a chicken house and pen along with a couple other small buildings. We bought a couple cows and about twentyfive chickens. AJ got busy organizing things while I was at work and doing any repairs that needed to be done. It was nice to come home from work and have him there. It was like we had traded places. I worked and he stayed at home. AJ got bored with staying home pretty quick. He went around and met some of the local farmers and he got offered a job driving one of the grain trucks for one of them. It didn't pay much but got him out of the house. I overheard him talking to a couple of the farmers and then I knew, he was telling them that I had gotten this promotion to move there and that he had planned on staying in Bentonville but him and his boss had been arguing and AJ was just fed up with it and quit his job. He decided at that point to move with me. I had thought all that time that he had moved because he loved me and didn't want to live apart but now, I knew the truth. It hurt but not as bad as it used to. I kept working and AJ added a garage to the house. Storm shelter installed, in the garage because Plainview was known for having tornadoes too. Once he got that done he started looking for a trucking job. He'd had his CDL for many years so that wouldn't be a problem. The problem ended up being there were no available jobs. He filled in for someone if they were out but that was far and few between. The farmers got to where they didn't need his help anymore and he couldn't get hired on at Walmart because I was a manager there and they couldn't have any favoritism. He could haul freight out of the DC but only as a dedicated driver. Meaning, he worked for another company that was hired by Walmart to move their freight.

AJ decided one day that he was going move motorhomes from state to state. He went to a class the company held and then he was off on the road to go pick up RVs'. He wasn't bringing in any money at first because he was just getting started. He had bought a new jeep that was as plain as you can get to haul behind the motorhomes so he would be able to move to the next job, then he had to pay to have the hitch put on the jeep. He also had to purchase the draw bar that went from the RVs to the jeep. Oh, and don't forget that we also had to purchase a laptop, a hot spot and a wireless printer so he could print out his jobs. I tried to tell him that he would be losing money by doing this, but I just couldn't convince him. He just knew that he would be able to make good money. He worked for a little while and realized he needed a different attachment to attach to the RVs so we had to pay for another one. I was making good money and paying all the bills, but I didn't mind because AJ had done the same thing when I stayed home with the girls but with all the expenses of getting set up to move the RVs was starting to really add up.

The RV moving lasted about nine months and AJ realized he wasn't making any money. One good thing came out of him moving those RVs though! I got to go on one of the trips with him and we went to New York and met my Aunt Donna for the very first time! We spent four or five days with her, and I asked her for all the old family stories she could remember! She's a beautiful woman with a heart of gold. She loves her children and welcomed us with open arms. I loved her the minute I saw her. The funny part was, I looked more like her than my own birth mother! Aunt Donna had five children, four girls and one boy. She had lived a rough life until she met her second husband. We met most of Aunt Donna's children and not one of them look alike! We didn't get to meet her son. He lives in Canada and teaches school there. I absolutely loved meeting my cousins and Aunt Donna. We had to get moving to get me back in time to go back to work. AJ went to work for one of the local guys, hauling loads out of or to different busines. I finally sold the house in Bentonville and decided to get a gastric bypass done. I was sick of hearing how fat I was and after every diet I had tried, I was desperate to have just taken care of. Work would not help cover any of my (sleeve) as they call it unless I had certain ailments. I had them all except diabetes. They refused to cover my surgery because I didn't have enough illness to meet their requirements?! How crazy is that! I got my sleeve done, and just a few months later, found out that I would be getting a promotion to Operations Manager. I was being moved back home to Ottawa Kansas where I had started out. We were both excited to be going home! We had been gone way too long and were ready. AJ had a few more runs that he needed to get done for his boss, but it was okay because with the promotion that I had gotten, Walmart sent people in that packed all my belongings and then moved them to a storage area until we were able to find a house. AJ's boss could be a little slow in paying so I told him to make sure he was paid before he did the next job. He did that for the next few jobs but then ran a couple that he didn't. He was asked to take the truck to a truck stop in Texas, so I had to drive down there from Kansas to pick him up. He never did get paid for those last two jobs or for delivering the tractor trailer to the truck stop and leaving it there. I found a house close to the golf course and we had them bring the furniture and got moved into our new home. I worked at Ottawa for about a year when I had to go out for surgery on my hands. It had gotten to the point that I couldn't write or type without considerable pain.

They were going to do one hand first and once that was out of the cast, they would do the other one. When they got in there, they discovered there was so much arthritis, it had eaten the bones up enough that they couldn't save the bones. They pulled a tendon from my arm and one from my hand, attached those to my thumb and then I had to learn how to use my hands all over again. Before I had made it off my medical leave, Walmart called me in for a meeting and informed me that my position had been eliminated. I could sign up for another position and start all over, or I could take a severance package. I chose the severance package. There was no way I would be able to go back out of the floor and work with my hands the way they were. Walmart was basically moving the people with any longevity out and bringing in new people. I wasn't the only one that was let go. There were several of us and I found out it was nationwide. I didn't know what to do with myself now. I had thrown myself into my job to help me cope with everything I was going through. I couldn't make any close friends because I didn't think I could handle being hurt again like I had been before.

We had bought a place in South Texas and when Walmart let me go on vacation for two weeks. I had found a house trailer plus the land it was on for sell. I used my 401 K to purchase it. AJ thought I was crazy but I knew my job was on the chopping block. "One of my acquaintances worked in the department in Bentonville, Arkansas had warned me that with my longevity, my job would be one that they were looking at to cut costs. Buying the trailer ended up being a blessing." we had to move out of the house as soon as possible so we could get it on the market. We would not be able to afford the house payment with me not having a job. Everything was packed in a hurry and what we didn't feel that we would be able to use or want, we took to the auction to be sold. My sister Sandy came down for a week and worked with me trying to get the trailer organized. I don't think I could have gotten it done without her help! She was a life saver! I ended up staying in Texas and AJ moved in with his second cousin. Every time I would talk to him on the phone, he would tell me about all the stuff they were doing. They went out to dinner at least a couple times a week, went to a country concert once or twice a month and he was always buying her things. He told me it was because he appreciated her letting him stay with her and she wouldn't let him pay any rent so that was his way of paying her back. He bought most all the groceries and did most of the cooking because she had warned him that she didn't cook. He redid all her land scaping, and His intentions were well meant, and I shouldn't have felt jealous, but I was, because he never did any of those things with or for me. It was almost like they were dating, and I was the outsider.

AJ came out to Texas right before Christmas and stayed January and February before he had to head back to Kansas for work. During the time he was in Texas, we got into several arguments and he said something to me for the very first time. He said that if I wasn't happy with our relationship then maybe we should just get divorced. I was shocked and hurt that our relationship didn't mean anymore to him than that. I felt that I had worked so hard to make our marriage work and given up so much, but he was just ready to throw it away. He mentioned divorce a few times during his time in Texas, but we managed to work most of it out. Once AJ left, more and more people started heading back to their summer homes. It was like the place was a ghost town. I was super lonely and hated being there by myself.

AJ's cousin and him, both decided that since I was so lonely, I should move back to Kansas and live with them too. She was even open to my pups being there, so I took off one day and went back to Kansas. It ended up being very difficult with two women in the house. She was used to it being just her and AJ and now when we went out, she was the third wheel. AJ and I were fighting quite a bit but trying to keep it away from his cousin. I kept telling him that it wasn't working for me and that I would be better off living in the motorhome. He could stay where he was, but I was used to having my own space and trying to live with another woman, no matter how much I loved her, was hard. AJ thought I was being silly and just causing problems but when our cousin decided to have a talk with me, she told me that I didn't do enough and that my not eating in the kitchen with them was rude. I explained that most of what they cooked made me feel nauseous so I would sit in the living room while they ate their dinner. She thought that was extremely rude and that I needed to get over it. She also told me that she felt like she had her daughter living with her (whom she had told us was a terrible person). Being told that, I just didn't feel comfortable staying there. I was very hurt by her saying that because I had tried my best to be polite and loving toward her because I did and do love her. She had told me that if I ever wanted to have anyone over, I was welcome to. She wanted us to treat the house as if it was our home too. I said something about inviting my oldest sister Sandy over but then was told to let her know when I was going to and she would make sure she left. Well, that didn't make me feel good about inviting anyone over. I didn't want her to feel like she had to leave her own home if I had company. If she had company come over, I would say hello and then I would take the pups and go to our room to give her, her privacy. The next day, she told me to ignore what she had said but I couldn't. I just didn't feel right about inviting anyone over after that. Things were rather tense, and I felt that I couldn't be myself or do what I wanted to. AJ was home on a Saturday and he overheard some of the things that were being said and noticed that his cousin was spending more and more time in her sewing room, like she wasn't comfortable in her own home. He said that we would move me out to the camper the next day. The following morning, we packed my stuff up and moved me to the camper. AJ spent the night. I made a dinner with enough left over for him to take to the house for him and his cousin. When he heated it up and served it, she refused to eat it. He asked her why and she said that her stomach was upset, and she just couldn't. He served it again the next night and again, she refused to eat it so he asked her why, is it because Kat made it? She said no that her stomach was just upset, and she couldn't eat. After that, he said she wouldn't come home at night until after she knew he would be asleep and wouldn't get up until after she knew he had left for work. I felt terrible and told him, he couldn't let that go on. She should feel comfortable in her own home and if she was doing that then he just needed to move out to the camper with me and let her have her house back. When we moved AJ out, she made us take almost everything that he had bought her plus all the groceries and even the mattress that we had replaced on the bed we were sleeping on. She said that when he bought those things for her, she felt as if he was telling her that her stuff wasn't good enough. I know, she knew better than that and that she was just angry. It hurt me to see her like that and I wished I had never moved in there in the first place. If I hadn't moved in, they would have just kept doing what they were doing and they were happy. I ruined that but it wasn't on purpose! I love her so much and it hurts that the relationship was ruined by my moving in. When I said something to AJ about all the stuff, he bought his cousin, and that he had never done any of those things for me, he got mad and asked me if I thought he didn't buy enough things for me. I didn't want to feel that way but no, he doesn't and hasn't bought stuff like that for me. If it was something that he wanted, then yes, we would purchase it. If it is something that I wanted but wasn't going to benefit him, then we didn't need it. In other words, AJs' wants were needs, my wants were just wants', and so they weren't needed.

With covid breaking out, no one was getting together and that kept everyone at home as much as possible. I had tried to call Tammie and Joe to make sure they were okay as I know they were older. It had been long enough that I just needed to get over how he was and move on. I had talked to Tammie over the phone, and she said that we needed to get together and play some games or go out for dinner or something. I told her that sounded good to me. I was out running some errands on day and decided that I needed to be the bigger person and make peace. I stopped and Tami's house first, but she was on the phone and said it was work so I told her I would wait in my truck until she was done. I waited around an hour and then she came back to the door and said that she would be on the phone for a lot longer. They were having trouble with something at work, and she wouldn't be able to talk to me. I think she was on the phone with Joe, and she wasn't ever going to talk to me. I ask for her phone number so I could call her, but she gave me a fake number. I guess she is still too much of a chicken to talk to me because she knows she did me dirty. I think she had planned all along to get Joe. She couldn't stand not being the center of attention. I left and then went over to Tammy and Joe's house to invite them to go out to dinner that evening if it would work. Joe was in the garage when I pulled up and I said hi. He stepped out of the garage and told me that I was unwelcome there. He said that "they had not seen or heard from me in fifteen to twenty years and had no use for me to be in their lives now. He asked why I hadn't ever called and of course, it was because of the way he had treated me, but I just told him that I didn't live in Kansas. I lived in another state most of the time. I far as I know, the phone works both ways and he had never made an effort to call me so what was the big deal?! He came at me in anger, but I stood my ground and he stepped back and just told me to leave. He didn't have any wish to see or have anything to do with us. I kind of gave him a smile, climbed into my truck and left. He blocked my phone number. I haven't heard or seen any of them. I have no idea what TamI told him to get him to act the way he did towards me but from my experiences with her, it could be anything. Everyone had always thought Tammie was the one that wasn't normal, but I think he had gotten just as bad if not worse than she was. Sam told me to stay away from them. That they had both gotten really crazy. He said that Joe used to invite him out to the lake house, but he hadn't heard from him in quite a while and when he hinted about going out to the lake house, the subject got changed. He was worried that they would do something stupid. They weren't really even friends anymore. I realized that Joe had never loved me. I met with his old friend for coffee, and he told me that Joe had never loved me. He just said he did so he would get lucky. He told me that they were all bad news, and to stay away from them. It just wasn't worth my trying to get back to being friends with them. Sam also asked if I would be interested in having a relationship with him, but I told him, I just couldn't. He is too much like a brother to me and I wouldn't be comfortable with anything but friendship. I had been in love with Joe, and it wasn't just a fling to me. I knew he wouldn't ever leave his wife and TamI must have figured that out too as she remarried her exhusband again. AJ and I have been working very hard on trying to make our relationship better. We still have our disagreements and must pay attention to what we say and do to not hurt the other person. I do still get my feelings hurt because AJ can say or do things without even thinking about it that is hurtful. I have gotten better about letting him know that I don't appreciate what he is saying or doing. I also have the house in Texas, and I have told him that I just won't do it anymore. If he can't treat me decent, then I will just pack up and move back to Texas. I came back at the end of February with him because he thought I should, but I hate the cold so much because it makes me hurt, I have informed him that I will be leaving for Texas this year before the cold hits and won't be coming back to Kansas until I know it's warm out. No more of the cold weather for me! I still feel like I am broken but I try every day to find something good about the world that I live in. I have lost almost all of my weight and am actually quite a bit smaller than AJ is now. We still have our arguments and when we went shopping, he got everything he wanted but everything I wanted to get, I was told we didn't need it. When we checked out, I noticed everything in the cart was for him and not one thing for me. When we got into the truck to head home, I told him I didn't know if he would ever catch on that I am an adult and don't need a father figure. He got mad and said that he just didn't seem to be able to make me happy and if that was the case, then we need to just get divorced. I told him that was fine. That was the fifth time that he had mentioned divorce in the last 9 to 10 months and if he wanted a divorce than that is what we would do. I wasn't going to fall apart and let him know how much he hurts me every time he does that. I took off my rings and started packing my stuff. He was shocked and started worrying about me leaving. I told him, he has said something about getting divorced about five times now and there will not be a sixth. If he ever says it again, I will be gone. I want to be with someone that wants and loves me. Not someone who uses me. We are together for now, and we will be married 50 years next month, but I don't know how long it will last. If it doesn't, then I'm sure there is someone out there that can love me for who I am and if not, then I will be okay on my own. I love him but I can't keep living with the constant hurt. I would be lonely, but I think I would be better off alone than with someone that doesn't love me. I feel like as long as I was bringing in the money, then all was good but now that I am on disability, I can't help as much financially as I did and that has been an adjustment. I don't know how many years I worked when he didn't but now that I can't work and am on a fixed income, things have changed. We put new appliances in the trailer in Texas and had to take out a loan to get them. He had me get the loan and his name is not on them. The same with the Can AM. Both our names are on the title, but I had to take out the loan and my name is the only one on it as well. It's almost like he is making sure that most of the money I get is spent so I won't have hardly anything to live on if I did leave. I could be way off on that but that's how it makes me feel. My hopes are that we can make things work and he will be able to show that he loves me. I would love nothing more than to grow old together with love and understanding and will still be holding hands into our twilight years.